Responsibly Spoken
A Manual for Public Speaking
and Business and Professional Speaking

Donald R. Thomas ▪ **Victor L. Blocher** ▪ **Donnell A. King**
Pellissippi State Technical Community College

KENDALL/HUNT PUBLISHING COMPANY
4050 Westmark Drive   Dubuque, Iowa 52002

Dedication

To our families and colleagues who supported us and challenged us in making this effort our best, and encourage us to continue to grow—to Janet, Zach, Amanda, Jon, Caty, Lauren, Victor, Brett, Brian, and Adam—and to our students for their input over the years.

Acknowledgments

We appreciate the time, effort, and support of our colleagues Dorothy Donaldson, Charles Miller, and Anita Maddox as we wrestled with and developed this edition.

We also want to thank and acknowledge copyeditor Mark Logan for his attention to detail and improvement (good catches!) and illustrator Todd Long for his insight into the speech process.

A portion of the proceeds of each new copy of this text that is sold goes to the Pellissippi State Foundation for speech communication and general scholarships.

Contents

Chapter 4
Ethics in Communication 33

Chapter 5
Audience Analysis 41

Chapter 6
Choosing Purposes and Topics 47

Chapter 7
Researching Your Speeches 65

Chapter 8
Principles of Organization 73

Chapter 9
Mechanics of Outlining 81

Chapter 10
Supporting Materials 93

Chapter 11
Language: Verbal Aspects of Public Speaking 107

Chapter 12
Delivery: Nonverbal Aspects of Public Speaking 119

Chapter 13
Delivery: Mechanics of Presenting to an Audience 135

Chapter 14

Informative Speeches 151

Chapter 15

Persuasive Speeches 157

Preface to the Third Edition

This book is about effective public speaking. Its approach is consciously chosen to act as "software for the brain."

Both of those are simple statements that can be complex in application.

For instance, consider the phrase "effective public speaking." Those three words comprise a human activity that has occupied the lives of countless scholars for thousands of years. Ask any of them what constitutes effective public speaking, and you will get countless (and often contradictory) answers.

Let's be clear, then, and say that by effective public speaking we mean speaking in front of groups of people in such a way as to help you achieve your purposes for speaking. Doing so gives us a simple gauge for success, therefore. For instance, if someone asks whether the use of profanity in a speech is a good thing or not, we can simply answer by saying, "Does it help you achieve your purpose? If so, it's a good thing. If not, it's a bad thing."

What about "software for the brain"? Simply put, we intend for this book to be a tool of genuine education. We say that not to pass judgment on other educators, but to remind both educators and readers about the intended outcome of education.

You see, many people think education consists of lining students up and essentially pouring information into their heads. The teacher at the front of the room is the "sage on the stage," the holder of knowledge who will transfer that knowledge to the students, whose job it is to absorb it. When they know what the teacher knows, the teacher has done his job. (See language note at the end of this section under the heading of "Conventions In This Book.")

Whatever that is, it's not education. The word comes

from the root *educe*, which means to draw forth. Information, facts, figures, research reports, all are part of education, but they are not the education itself—they are the *tools* of education. You use those tools to draw something forth from yourself: your ability to think and reason, your skills, your potential.

This text, then, is not designed simply to give you information *about* effective public speaking, but to give you tools with which to draw forth your own unique skills and abilities and use them in your own unique situations by the application of universal principles. Graduation represents not an ending, but a beginning, as commencement speakers constantly tell us. They are right. When you have finished this course, we hope you will find this textbook worth keeping, because we hope it will help you to continue to develop and hone your skills in communicating with others in your life.

As Anita Maddox, a colleague of ours, told me in a conversation, "If you're not taught to think and reason on your feet out loud, critically, that's the beginning of the end of the republic. You cannot participate outside your own field. You can't discover new ideas within the fields of others because you can't evaluate what you hear. What Aristotle talked about, the process of rhetoric, the discovery in any case all the available means of persuasion—that's the foundation of every institution and system in our country."

This, then, is not the only software you need for your brain. But it's a pretty good start.

Conventions in This Book

The English language is still evolving and has not yet come up with a personal pronoun that is gender neutral. "It" is too impersonal. "Their" is plural and doesn't fit with a singular subject. Constant uses of "his/her" and "s/he" gets awkward. Where it is possible to do so without slipping into ridiculous constructions, we will structure sentences so as to avoid third-person singular pronouns. Where it is not possible, or at least inadvisable, we will honor the mix of readership by alternating the gender.

Also, please realize this book results from longterm collaboration among three primary authors, with contributions occasionally from colleagues. Parts of the book uses "I" where "we" or "one of the authors" could be awkward. It's just easier sometimes.

Chapter 1

Introduction to Speech Communication Study

By definition communication is a conscious or unconscious process by which feelings and ideas are expressed in verbal and nonverbal messages. According to social scientists, human beings constantly send out and receive messages in a variety of ways. Social scientists have identified that 15 percent of our communication time is spent in reading, 11 percent in writing, 32 percent as senders of messages and 42 percent as receivers of messages (listeners).

Because we spend so much of our time receiving messages, it makes sense to consider the importance of the entire communication loop. For the communication process to succeed, the message must be received as well as sent. Communication is a two-way process. When we speak, we do not necessarily communicate unless the message is received and also understood. Action and reaction forms the foundation for all communication.

The Great Britain ferry sinking illustrates this clearly. In 1980 a ferry left port from Great Britain into the English Channel. Shortly after the ferry sank as a result of the rear tail gate being left open (in a down position). Communication analysts agree that the message was indeed transmitted to the second mate to raise the back gate. What is uncertain is why the message wasn't understood by the second mate. Communication analysts theorize that "message static" was potentially to blame.

"**Message Static**" is defined as vocabulary differences (semantics), message interference, technical

What Is Communication?

[Editor's note: One of the authors has given the following as a handout in class for several years. It adds some perspective to the rest of the material in this chapter.]

Before you read any further, take a moment to fill in here what communication means to you.

_____

_____

Go ahead, fill it in. We know you skipped over it.

Now that you have thought about what communication means to you, compare it to this scholarly definition:

"Communication is a transactional process involving a cognitive sorting, selecting, and sending of symbols in such a way as to help a listener elicit from his or her own mind a meaning or response similar to that intended by the communicator" (Ross, 11).

Huh?

Go back and look at it again, and let's take it apart a bit. You'll find that there are a lot of similarities between what you said, and what Ross said. There may also be some important differences.

First, a transactional process. There are some implications there. Transaction means a back-and-forth, a give-and-take. It goes both ways. Even in public speaking, communication is a two-way street. The speaker may be the most active, but the audience is constantly sending back to the speaker in the form of feedback.

And, it is a process. That is, it has no definite beginning point and no definite ending point (for instance, does it stop when the speaker has finished speaking? when the listener has understood it? when the listener has responded?), and the "steps," although they may appear to be distinct, actually overlap and happen all at the same time. In other words, it's complicated.

"A cognitive" means that it happens in your mind. We're dealing with what goes on in your head, not with what happens in reality, "out there." Alan Cohen tells of a worker in a rail yard who went to work on a freezer car. He accidentally got locked in. Other workers found him the next morning, dead. He had written on the wall, "Colder... getting so cold." But the freezer car was out of commission—the man had died because he had convinced himself that he was freezing to death! (Cohen, 231). What goes on in our minds affects our behavior, feelings, attitudes and actions far more than whatever might be "out there."

"Sorting, selecting, and sending of symbols" is the heart of communication. Unless you are psychic, you do not send or transmit ideas —a very common occurrence in students' definitions. You send a symbol which stands for an idea. When you see the word "dog," you are actually looking at a symbol two steps removed from the object it stands for in reality. D stands for a certain sound, O stands for a certain sound, and G stands for a certain sound. Put them all together, and you have "dog" (make the sound out loud, and just put up with the strange looks of those around you), a sound which in turn stands for an object in reality. You also get a picture in your mind. Chances are that picture comes from your own experience, and your picture will be different from my picture because our experience is different. If we transmitted ideas, we would have identical pictures. We will never have identical experiences, though, because I send a symbol that represents my idea, and you relate that symbol to a similar idea you already have in your head.

That it is already in your head is implied by the "in such a way as to help a listener elicit from his or her own mind a meaning or response similar to that intended by the communicator" part. Think about the impossibility of telling someone who has been blind from birth about a rainbow. It is impossible because you do not share the experience.

Around the turn of the century the Bible was translated into the Inuit language, a language spoken by a group of eskimoes who live their entire lives north of the Arctic circle. In the New Testament the phrase "lamb of God" appears quite often, a phrase that gave the translators a lot of trouble, because there was no word for "lamb" in Inuit. Why would there be? They had never seen one. They had no experience with sheep; why would they have any words for dealing with them? The translators tried to solve this problem by using a phrase which meant literally "a small animal that is like a caribou calf." That sort of got it across, except that the phrase in the New Testament has implications about meekness and gentleness that just doesn't get across via a comparison to caribou.

In the early 1990s a new translation was made into Inuit, one that didn't have this difficulty because there is now a word for "lamb" in Inuit. No, they still don't have sheep. But they do have satellite dishes. Therefore they have experienced sheep (without the accompanying odors) and the language now has a word for it.

Scholars express this in the saying, "Meaning is not in words; meaning is in people."

But, you say, words *must* have meaning. My dictionary tells me what a word means.

A dictionary only records how people *use* words. When a new dictionary is compiled, editors will send out, for instance, 5,000 index cards and ask 5,000 people to write down how they use the word "dog." Out of the 5,000, probably 4,000 will say something about a four-legged animal with a tail that barks, or some variant of that. And that will become the number one definition (in most dictionaries, the order of the definitions is significant; the lower the number, the more common its usage). But there will be a few dozen, perhaps, who will say that "dog" means to fasten, as in "dog a hatch" (these people probably spent a lot of years in the navy). Some people will say it means to bother, as in "quit dogging me, man!" Maybe one card will say it means "my mother-in-law." That one won't go in the dictionary, not because it's "wrong," but because not enough people use the word that way for it to be recorded.

But that doesn't mean the one person doesn't use the word that way. It doesn't mean that you wouldn't understand him if he did. If you knew him you would know how he used the word. You would also be able to tell from the context in which he used the word. If I say, "Let's go down to the cafeteria and chow down on a dog," do you need a dictionary to figure out what I mean? It is more important to determine how someone is using a word (at least, more important for clear communication) than to determine who is using it "correctly."

Trick question: did the word "broadcast" appear in an English dictionary in 1810?

Not-so-trick answer: yes. People used the word differently, of course. It meant "a method of sowing seed." It is still listed that way in an unabridged dictionary, although it is certainly not the first definition. (For those who don't know, broadcast of seeds involves scattering them widely, not putting them in a particular place.)

So dictionaries just record how a large number of people use a symbol. That's why dictionaries change, because people change the way they use words.

Look at a map. How do you know what the symbols mean? You can find out from the "key." There is no inherent meaning in any symbol. The only connection between, say, k and a capital city is that "negotiated" or defined by the map maker.

Words are the same way. We don't *think* of them that way, because when as children we ask "what is this," our parents don't say, "We use the sound 'pen' to stand for that object, honey." They say, "This *is* a pen," as if the sound is an inherent characteristic of the object. The French may *call* it something else, but *we* know it *is* a pen.

Ever notice how Americans behave when in a foreign country, one where they don't speak the local language and the locals don't speak English? How do they attempt to communicate? Aside from gestures (which make sense sometimes), most Americans will attempt to communicate by continuing to speak English, but they speak slower and louder. "Where is the bathroom? WHERE ... IS ... THE ... BATHROOM? WHERE ...... IIIISSSS .... THE ..... BAAAATTH ...... ROOOOOM?" The idea seems to be, "If I just say this slow enough and loud enough, this idiot will understand." Can we see from this that words are just symbols, to which we attached commonly agreed-upon meanings?

Among the implications for communication: we tend to assume that if I use the right words and you don't understand them, then it's "your fault" if you don't understand. But when we realize that meaning is in people, not in words, we can take full responsibility for effective communication wherever we might happen to be in the "formula."

(See accompanying CD for color model of process.)

problems or incongruency of shared meaning of signs and symbols. Semantics is the study of language meanings. Meanings do not reside in the words themselves, but are determined by the receivers. When people use language differently from the way you do, it is because their experiences differ from yours—not good or bad, wrong or right, just different. This difference explains why translators are required between cultures with different dialects of the same "language."

Communication in Business

Just as communication is important on an interpersonal level, it is also very important that organizations or businesses communicate in an efficient, articulate manner. Failure to make your point quickly in business communication can lead to lost business and revenue. Organizational communication failure can sabotage chances for a successful sale, limit career advancement, or bog down an otherwise good business organization. A good manager must connect with all segments of an organization and receive comprehensive feedback. Thus, as a manager or as

Figure 1.1: Organization chart

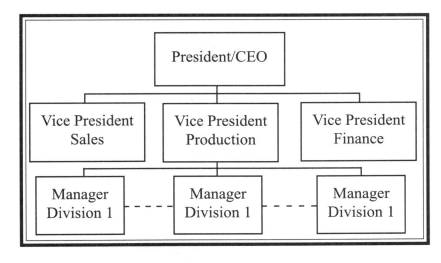

7

a subordinate you must communicate both internally (with people in your business) and externally (with people and clients outside your business).

Organizations often develop formal channels of communication to ensure feedback both downward and upward in the organization. This is called an Organizational Chart or "Org. Chart." An Org. Chart is defined as a formal communication system of communication both formal and informal. **Org. Charts are established** for both giving and receiving assignments and **for determining who is whose boss.**

A generic "org. chart" to ensure precise reporting and articulate communications should be more or less designed as indicated in Figure 1.1.

Organizational charts streamline business activity and ensure a better working corporate machine.

Communication static was to blame for the Pearl Harbor disaster. It was also to blame (at least to some degree) for the dropping of the atomic bomb on Hiroshima and Nagasaki.* Message static may also prove disastrous in the workplace, if your boss gives you an assignment but you fail to understand what he or she really wants you to do.

---

*Col. Ralph Capio has said in "The Atomic Bombings of Japan: A 50-Year Retrospective" that the Japanese were on the verge of starvation and ready to surrender, but hesitated because of perceived ambiguity regarding the emperor's status after an "unconditional surrender." "In response to the Potsdam Declaration, the Japanese government issued a statement to its people, which led to one of history's most consequential 'failures to communicate.' While posturing with the Russians, the Japanese suggested that they were 'withholding comment' on the Potsdam Declaration. From reports in Japanese newspapers, the United States concluded that the Japanese believed that the declaration was of 'no great value' and was being 'ignored.' Taking this response to be a rejection, Truman ordered that the atomic bombs be dropped as a means of ending the war promptly (and on favorable terms) and of 'influencing' Stalin."

Communication is the way relationships are maintained. Communication is irreversible. It is impossible to undo a message once it is sent. A slip of the tongue or an emotional outburst is impossible to erase and is a meaningful glance into a speaker's true feeling. We may deny or apologize, but that does not eradicate what has taken place.

> **Communication is irreversible. It is impossible to undo a message once it is sent.**

Audience Demographics

Understanding what type of people are in the audience and what their likes and dislikes are is important. The process of determining these types, likes, and dislikes is called demographics. **The study of demographics is the study of the socioeconomic aspects, the age, the race, the religion, the biases, the likes and dislikes of the selected audience.** In other words, the speaker finds out more about his target audience than he ever needs to know. Demographics may be utilized in the public speaking forum or in conversation (both casual or formal).

Study questions
1. Why do we say communication is a transactional process? *speaker is active, but the audience sends feedback back*
2. What percentage of our time is spent in listening? *42 %*
3. What is the significance of "communication static"? *it is irreversible*

Works Cited in Chapter

Capio, Ralph J. "The Atomic Bombings of Japan: A 50-Year Retrospective." *Aerospace Power Chronicles.* Originally published in *Airpower Journal* (summer 1995). 22 May 2002 <http://www.airpower.maxwell.af.mil/airchronicles/apj/capio.html>.

Cohen, Alan. *I Had It All the Time.* Haiku, Hawaii: Alan Cohen Publications, 1995.

Ross, Raymond S. *Speech Communication: Fundamentals and Practice.* Englewood Cliffs, N.J.: Prentice-Hall, Inc., 1977.

Chapter 2

Your First Speech

The process of preparing a speech is divided into three phases: **Planning, Organization,** and **Delivery.**

As with any new activity the speechmaking process may seem alien to you at first. **But by proceeding in a logical order and by following a prescribed plan, you, the novice speaker, can perform well your first time at the lectern.** By paying attention to your speech-making process, you can begin building good organizational habits that are necessary for effective speaking.

When you begin to prepare a speech, you have to look closely at your overall organizational patterns. Below is a plan for making a speech. The process is logical and is listed step-by-step. As you gain familiarity with the process, adapt it to your own use. But be careful and take your time. **Understand this process completely before tailoring it to your own use.**

Planning

There are five steps in the planning phase of the speech: deciding the purpose for speaking, selecting a topic, researching the topic, creating a thesis, and defining major terms and phrases.

Depending on the individual circumstances of your speaking situation, the steps may come in any order within the planning phase. The ordering of the steps is of secondary importance to the need to complete each step before you move on to the next phase.

Step 1—Purpose, General and Specific

Deciding the purpose of the speech helps you understand:

- **why** you are giving the speech,
- **what** you hope to accomplish,
- **what** you want your audience to remember, believe, or act upon.

You should always select one overriding general purpose.

General Purpose. Your general purpose determines the overall type of speech you give. You may have more than one purpose for speaking, and your speech may be a combination of speech types, but in order to focus on what you are saying and who you are saying it to, you should always select one overriding general purpose.

Three major categories for general purposes for speaking are **to inform, to entertain,** and **to persuade**. Each of these may have subcategories. For instance, subcategories of informative speeches include **to demonstrate** and **to teach**. Subcategories of persuasive purposes are highly dependent on the demographic make-up of your audience and include **to make in-roads, to convince,** or **to actuate.**

There are other, more specific, purposes for speaking such as to propose a toast to someone or something, to present a testimonial or a eulogy, or to sermonize. These speeches rarely require the research or the formal organization of other extemporaneous speaking, however.

Specific Purpose. Your specific purpose is much more concrete in scope. It tells you exactly what response you hope to elicit from your audience upon completion of your speech. For instance, if your topic is automobile safety and your general purpose is to actuate, then your specific purpose might be to get your audience members to wear their seatbelts.

Audience members judge your speech in part by how well you satisfy your specific purpose. To effectively understand your specific purpose, complete the following sentence (you use this sentence in our outline under *specific purpose* in Chapter 9).

At the end of my speech I want my audience to

_____ .

Step 2—Topic

The topic of your speech is the subject of your speech. It is what you are talking about. Your general topic is a broad category of knowledge about a specific field. Usually you must decide upon and research a broad topic before you narrow that topic to a thesis sentence. Just choosing a topic is not enough to begin organizing a speech. Before you get to the actual organization of the speech, you must decide which part of your topic to emphasize based upon your purpose for speaking and your research.

Often a group will ask a speaker to speak on a certain topic—something the speaker is familiar with, a cause that is dear to the speaker, an expertise that the speaker possesses—but usually the speaker chooses his own purpose and topic. **The speaker always tailors his own thesis.**

What criteria must a speaker use when choosing a topic?

You must first understand the parameters of your speaking forum by asking questions such as:

☐ What interests do my audience and I have in common?

☐ What topics do I feel comfortable with?

☐ What is the speaking environment (length of speech, declared purpose of the speech, demographics of the audience, type of speaking space)?

☐ How much preparation time can I devote to the project?

If you are still stumped, consider everyday activities and interests. Ask yourself:

☐ What do I really like to do?

☐ What is important to me?

☐ What catches my interest?

☐ What really irritates me?

You needn't get too specific when working in the preliminary stages of deciding on your topic and beginning your preliminary research. You may only have a broad topic at first which requires research before a direction becomes apparent.

Step 3—Research

Part of the speaker's ethical responsibility is to tell the truth as he or she knows it, based on competent investigation. So you will want to spend a good deal of the planning phase finding competent authorities to support your reasoning and to supply your evidence. Usually some research is necessary before deciding how to narrow your topic into a thesis sentence.

More research may be necessary throughout the speech planning process, but the preliminary research at this step should be the most comprehensive.

Step 4—Thesis Sentence

By definition, **a thesis sentence is a simple declarative statement with a provable generality.**

The core of the thesis is "simple" in structure, having no added clauses or unnecessary phrases. Usually the subject of the thesis statement is the topic of the speech. The predicate (verb) of the statement represents the direction in which you, the speaker have taken your topic, or how you have narrowed it. A "provable generality" means an idea or concept that must be demonstrated as true using hard evidence and reasoning. The statement is "declarative" (it ends in a period, not a question mark).

A formal piece of composition—whether oral or written—is based on the idea of communicating one primary thought: the thesis (also called the central idea, hypothesis, topic sentence).

The thesis sentence is the essence of the speech. It is the idea that is proven by the main points of the body of the speech. **The thesis sentence is the one thought that you want your audience to remember and accept.**

The rest of the speech is designed only to support the thesis. No matter how well you deliver your speech, no matter how cleverly you explain your examples, no matter how thoroughly you have researched your topic, you will not present a good speech without a strong thesis. You should, therefore, spend time developing the exact wording of your thesis and understanding its ramifications.

> **If the thesis is weak, then the speech cannot fulfill the purpose of communicating a central idea, and the purpose for speaking is lost.**

Having a strong thesis gives the speech direction, meaning that the speech makes a point. If the thesis is weak, then the speech cannot fulfill the purpose of communicating a central idea, and the purpose for speaking is lost.

Step 5—Definition

Careful use of definition at this step can save hours of confusion later. Remember, the definitions you use are yours, and they are designed only for the specific speech you are making. Many times you will need to explain your definitions in the clarification step of the introduction on your outline.

Sometimes even the most obvious words need defining. In the thesis "Smoking is hazardous to your health," the term "smoking" may appear to you to be self-evident: smoking cigarettes. However, there are many things that can be smoked and many ways of smoking. Let's say you are speaking of the carcinogenic dangers of smoking fish or turkey on the grill. The thesis still makes sense, but it takes on an entirely different meaning.

Likewise, a speech on the dangers of smoking a pipe or a cigar presents different arguments than does a speech on smoking cigarettes. Therefore, "smoking" would need to be defined for your audience

All major terms in your thesis statement need definition, even if their meaning seems obvious. You may never mention their definitions out loud, but a review of the meaning of each term by you at this point in planning your speech keeps your logic clear and definite.

Warning: You make a mistake if you use a general-purpose dictionary as your primary source of definitions. Lexicographers (people who write dictionaries) are not experts in the fields of the words they are cataloging. They simply record common usages of words at a specific time and list them in the order from most common to least common. In other words, they record how people use words, not necessarily how experts use words.

You should use specialty dictionaries or textbooks if you need an authoritative meaning for one of your major terms. Use the general-purpose dictionary to give you an idea and then consult an authority to give you a concrete definition for your speech.

Remember, you can define the word yourself for your specific need in the speech. If your definition is uncommon or has been tailored too much to fit your need, you may need to take time to explain your definition to your audience. The stranger the definition, the more you will have to work to convince your audience to accept it.

Delivering Your Speech

You will find yourself tempted to sound the way you think a speaker is supposed to sound. Don't. Speaking is not about performing, it's about connecting with your audience and getting your idea across.

The best way to accomplish this is to think in terms of having a conversation with audience members. We'll talk later about **conversational delivery**. The idea is *not* to sound just exactly as you do in conversation, because most people wander around a lot, use incomplete sentences, vocalize pauses, etc., in actual conversation. Rather, we're talking about the way the delivery feels to the audience.

For instance, we want to strongly emphasize in every way possible in print the following idea: ***DO NOT READ OR MEMORIZE YOUR SPEECH.*** You have been on the receiving end of such performances. You *know* how deadly dull such can be. Don't inflict that pain on your audience or on yourself.

Here's another way to put it: while you should rehearse your speech for the sake of familiarity, don't worry about trying to get the words exactly right in front of the audience. Weeks from now they won't remember the exact words you used, only the impression you created with them. Thus, the language (and everything else you use) is a means to the end of affecting the audience, not the end in itself. So rehearse the speech to be comfortable with the order in which you're presenting the ideas, the ideas themselves, and the visual aids you might use. But don't worry about getting everything exactly right. It is much more important to *connect* with the audience and be ready to adapt to their reactions.

For the same reason, ***DO NOT WRITE OUT YOUR SPEECH WORD FOR WORD***. In addition to what we've already said, we should point out that people don't talk the way they write. If you ever write your speech out word for word it will sound like you're reading it *even when you're not*. Plan and organize, certainly; rehearse, absolutely. But don't write it out. Use an outline like a map, and make brief notes to remind you of what you want to say. Then just say it.

Summary

The first phase of making a speech, then, consists of five steps. These steps may vary in order depending on the individual speaking circumstance, but you should be satisfied that you have concrete information for each of the first five steps before continuing to the next phase. Remember that a speech is more like a dance with the audience than like a military march. Plan ahead, but go with the actual events.

Measuring Speechfright

To demonstrate that your speechfright symptoms will diminish considerably by the end of the semester, we have devised a measurement to help you assess yourself.

Directions:

1. In the five spaces below, write your most noticeable speechfright symptoms.
2. Rate each symptom on a scale of 1–10 (the maximum amount of discomfort would rate a 10; the least amount would rate a 1).
3. At the end of the term turn to the similar form in Chapter 18 (Bonus material and appendices) and fill it out again. Then compare this one and that one to see the difference.

Initial observed symptom	Rating
1. _____	____
2. _____	____
3. _____	____
4. _____	____
5. _____	____

Sample:

Initial observed symptom	Rating
1. *Cotton mouth*	7
2. *Red face*	5
3. *Stuttering*	10
4. *Forgetfulness*	9
5. *Sweaty palms*	10

Study questions

1. What are the five steps in the first phase of making a speech?
2. What are the three major categories for general purposes?
3. What is a thesis sentence?
4. Explain what "conversational delivery" means.

Chapter 3

Speech Anxiety

Your palms are sweating, your pulse is racing, your knees are shaking. Are you going to your first job interview? Are you coming down with a serious illness? No, you are experiencing a physical and emotional reaction to talking before a group of people. You're experiencing speechfright—a normal response, a fear often felt by even the most knowledgeable and experienced speakers.

Speechfright, the fear of speaking before a group, is common to almost everyone. To some extent, we all feel uncomfortable standing while others are sitting, being stared at, and being "judged" by other people. An often-quoted study found that Americans feared public speaking more than just about anything else, including death or serious illness (Bruskin). A poll conducted for the National Communication Association found that only 24 percent of Americans are "very comfortable" giving a speech, and only 34 percent are "very comfortable" speaking up at a meeting (Roper-Starch).

Americans fear public speaking more than just about anything else.

While you may never be able to overcome this nervousness, you can learn to change some of the feelings of dread into feelings of anticipation and even excitement. In other words, you can learn to *harness* the energy. We don't really want to get rid of it.

You have something important to say. Assume your audience knows that and is eager to listen to you and to learn something from you. Most likely you have been asked to make this talk, so your audience is looking forward to your presentation. Even if you have sought this opportunity to present information or ideas, your audience will appreciate your efforts, will respect your knowledge, and will be supportive of you.

Fight-or-Flight Syndrome

Many thousands of years ago our early ancestors roamed the earth having to fight for their very lives every day. When they awakened in the morning, they had to kill or be killed by the very beasts that might become their dinner. Emotionally and physically our ancestors had to rise to the occasion to kill or be killed. Psychologists identify this response as the "fight-or-flight response," "fight" meaning to physically or psychologically fight the prehistoric beast or other danger and "flight" meaning to physically flee from the stressful situation.

The fight-or-flight syndrome is not merely a mental state, but evokes an increase in blood pressure and respiration and the excretion of the endocrine glands and the adrenal glands. When the impulse is sent to these glands, at once adrenaline is blasted into the blood stream. At the same moment, a trigger is pulled that shoots glycogen (a special form of blood sugar) from the liver into the blood stream. When these powerful secretions reach the heart, it starts pounding. When they hit the respiratory center in the brain, the victim starts to gasp. When these hormones hit the blood vessels going to the brain, they contract and wooziness occurs.

Less obvious effects are even more profound. Blood is drawn away from the internal organs and transferred to the large outer muscles—arms, legs, etc.— and as a result the digestive process is slowed down or stopped altogether. The blood clots more easily. Muscles become tense all through the body, and tense throat muscles tend to produce a harsh and constricted voice. Salivary glands stop secreting, the mouth becomes dry, and the tongue feels thick. In contrast, the sweat glands increase secretion until beads of perspiration stand on the forehead and the skin becomes moist. Breathing, of course, is difficult and short and jerky.

These reactions had value in terms of helping humans cope with physical danger. You were prepared to either fight or run. The problem for speakers is two-fold: the part of your brain that takes care of the perception of danger works *prior* to the reasoning part. For survival, that makes a lot of sense. Your reasoning abilities are powerful, but they don't work quickly enough to respond to actual danger. By the time you reasoned out a response, you

Illustration by Todd Long

would be dead. For speaking, though, this causes a problem. You can reason to yourself all you want that you shouldn't be afraid. It's too late. If your brain has perceived danger, it will kick in the fight-or-flight response. All of this takes place in a very short time in the body of one who is afflicted by speechfright in its extreme form.

The other problem is that in most speech situations you cannot do what your body is most prepared to do. It's generally considered bad form to run. It's very bad form to punch audience members. The result can be similar to sitting at a traffic light with your foot on the brake and the accelerator at the same time. Of course you're going to shake!

In milder forms, the body undergoes fewer changes, and the person feels "queazy," has faint disagreeable sensations, or is simply keyed up and tense.

Speechfright evokes in all speakers the fight-or-flight syndrome to some extent. A biographer observed at

23

George Washington's first inaugural that he was so "visibly perturbed that his hands trembled and his voice shook so that he could scarcely be understood." Abraham Lincoln suffered from speechfright all his life. When he rose to speak, he "froze in his tracks and he had a far away prophetic look in his eyes." Even Cicero, who lived in the century before Christ, experienced speechfright and left a record of his inner struggle in the words of Crassus: "I turn pale at the outset of a speech, and quake in every limb and in all my soul." It was said of Nathaniel Hawthorne that he was drenched in cold perspiration at the very thought of speaking at a banquet. John Dryden described his sensations: "Whenever I speak a cold sweat trickles down all over my limbs as if I were dissolving in water."

Remember that there is nothing weird, unnatural, or abnormal about being afraid to speak before others. Speechfright is the manifestation of your inner emotions and feelings. It is the body's way of preparing you emotionally and physically for a higher level of performance. Athletes call this response "the butterflies."

Dealing with Speechfright

Under the pressure of giving a speech you may not be able to remember a lot of specific things to do to assuage speechfright. However, you can probably remember a few specific things, and you can remember the underlying principles of dealing with it.

We want to do two basic things: stop the build-up of the adrenaline and other fight-or-flight chemicals, and deal with the adrenaline that is already present.

Build-up

For most people it's not the adrenaline that's the

problem, but rather the vicious cycle of adrenaline build-up. It generally works like this:

> *As you stand up to give your speech, you feel uncomfortable and vaguely threatened, so your body responds by shooting some adrenaline into your bloodstream to prepare you to fight or run. You do neither, but you have all that excess energy which causes your hands and knees to shake a bit. Because you can* feel *the shaking, you assume the audience can see it, although they really can't. "They know I'm scared," you think to yourself, which makes you feel more threatened, which shoots more adrenaline into your blood, which makes you shake more, which makes you feel more exposed, which makes you feel more threatened, which . . . .*

Speechfright is the body's way of preparing you emotionally and physically for a higher level of performance.

You can see the problem. Some of our techniques, then, simply interrupt this vicious cycle.

Once you've interrupted the cycle, though, you still have to deal with the adrenaline that is already in your blood. You certainly need a positive mental attitude to succeed as a speaker, and PMA helps stop the cycle, but PMA alone won't simply make the adrenaline go away.

If you've ever had too much to drink, and then (for whatever reason) suddenly needed to be sober, you know that just thinking about it doesn't make it so. The alcohol is in your blood, and it will metabolize at its own rate, regardless of your wishes. Drinking coffee won't get someone sober—you'll just have a wide-awake drunk on your hands.

Fortunately, adrenaline (and the related stress chemicals) was designed to be used by your body. You can, therefore, affect the rate of absorption and channel how it is used. Some of our techniques enable you to either "burn off" or harness the energy supply that adrenaline represents.

Warm Your Hands

In the fight-or-flight response the blood supply is drawn away from the smaller blood vessels, muscles, and bone structure. As a result the blood supply leaves the feet and hands and travels to the brain, heart, and other major organs and muscles. This response prepares an individual for the exerting/stressful occasion at hand. Those experiencing the flight or fight syndrome usually have cool or cold hands and feet. Hence, we have coined the term "cold hands." Researchers have found that by helping the hands to warm up, the flight or fight response is diminished considerably, thus helping the speaker to induce self-relaxation techniques which reduce speechfright. This interrupts the build-up cycle, and allows you to metabolize the excess adrenaline.

PMA alone won't simply make the adrenaline go away.

Warming the hands helps relax the speaker and has a tendency to offset the fight-or-flight syndrome by allowing the blood to flow in a more normal pattern of warmth and increased relaxation.

Here are some ways to warm your hands:

1. Sit on your hands.
2. Rub your cold hands together briskly.
3. Fold your arms in front and under each other.
4. Deeply breathe into your cupped hands.

Know Your Subject Matter

Knowing your subject matter and focusing on your research findings help in the relaxation process. For example, invariably when a student gets *emotionally involved* in the actual presentation of the speech regarding such topics as abortion, the death penalty, or religion or politics, all or some of the speechfright symptoms sail out the window. This fits with a bumper-sticker philosophy summary of this principle: "What you focus on, you get more of." If you focus on the speechfright, it will increase. Focus on your message. When you focus on your message, you don't focus on yourself, and you get more familiarity with the message.

The concentration is centered on the message and the research—and not on the speechfright or nervousness.

Joe still lived with his mom. One day Joe was cooking pancakes for breakfast. He really liked pancakes, got distracted by the wonderful smell as they cooked up on the griddle, and in his distraction reached for the unprotected handle of the cast iron griddle. He burned his hand and screamed out in pain. "Mom, Mom, I burnt my hand cooking these pancakes!" he cried. His mom came over to the stove, grabbed a frying pan and bashed Joe over the head with it! As Joe came to his senses, he asked his mom, "Why did you bash me with that skillet?" She said, "You forgot about your burnt hands, didn't you?"

Focus on What You *Want*

Many speakers focus on the very thing they want to get rid of. Your mind cannot really think in negative terms, however. We can illustrate that with an old trick: don't think about a pink elephant. Don't think about it! If you just focus on not thinking about a pink elephant, can you think about anything else?

If you want to be rid of the pink elephant, think about a green monkey instead.

> **Audiences really do "pull" for speakers and want them to do well.**

In the same way, if you are thinking, "Don't be scared, don't be scared," you're just thinking about being scared. What you focus on you get more of. Is that what you want? When you as a speaker truly focus your attention on the issue or task at hand, all speechfright symptoms will be forgotten or diminished appreciably.

Does it sound easier already? It should, because speaking before a group is seldom as stressful as you think it is going to be, especially once you start talking. Audiences really do "pull" for speakers and want them to do well. Once you see the friendly faces of the group turned toward you, your smiles returned by the audience, and their nods indicating support, agreement, or understanding, most likely you will automatically relax a bit and may even enjoy the experience. If you are one of the few speakers whose speechfright does not diminish as you progress through your talk, you can learn to deal with the discomfort at whatever stage the speechfright is most intense.

Have a Conversation

In fact, an easy technique that helps both your delivery and your speechfright is to pick out three or four (in a wider or fan-shaped audience, pick out five or six) people who are actively engaged with you (that is, they're looking back, smiling, nodding) and have a conversation with them. The others are welcome to eavesdrop. When you're sitting in the school or company cafeteria having a conversation, other friends drift up and you will naturally include them in the conversation. You will also include other audience members, but you can start with those few.

Susan Jeffers, in her book *Feel the Fear and Do It Anyway*, says she uses this technique quite often. She has learned to think of audiences as "friends I haven't met yet," which changes her whole approach.

You may wonder that if speechfright is common even to experienced speakers, how is it that they rid themselves of these symptoms? **Professional speakers have simply learned to deal with speechfright and to channel its energy into an enthusiastic, confident delivery.** If you don't think of it as something to get rid of, as something you actually want to cultivate (like being up for a basketball game), it doesn't feel bad. Many people pay good money to engage in such things as attending scary movies, riding roller coasters, going bungie jumping, driving race cars and other activities for the thrill associated with "getting the adrenaline pumping." You can speak for free! In fact, other people will pay *you* to do it!

Realistically, you can hope to alleviate your symptoms of speechfright during the next few weeks by:

1. Identifying your feelings and symptoms.
2. Realizing that nearly all speakers experience the same feelings.

3. Learning ways to cope with your individual symptoms by participating in several "desensitizing activities."
4. Practicing the delivery of several types of speeches in the mirror and utilizing a tape recorder.
5. Choosing an interesting subject.
6. Mastering your subject thoroughly.
7. Thinking about your audience and your subject, not about yourself.
8. Using some physical action while you speak.
9. Remembering that some nervous tension is necessary for good public speaking.
10. Speaking at every opportunity.
11. Thinking of your audience as individuals, not as a mass.
12. Developing a positive mental attitude (PMA).
13. Warming your hands before the speech.
14. Faking it until you make it.
15. Using humor.
16. Smiling.
17. Breathing deeply (breathe in slowly for 15 seconds; breathe out slowly for 15 seconds).

> **If you act scared, the audience will feel uncomfortable.**

You as a speaker must rid your mind of the mistaken notion that your listeners will get a good warm feeling out of seeing you embarrassed or ill at ease.

As Dr. Batsell Barrett Baxter pointed out several years ago, you can do a great deal to substitute confidence for fear by acting as if you feel confident. You can change depression into exhilaration by throwing back your shoulders, standing erect and speaking in a strong and pleasant voice. You really are happier when you are smiling than when you are frowning. Physiologists have long maintained that it takes more energy to frown than to smile.

The governess in *The King and I* uttered a profound truth when she said that she whistled when she was afraid, and that by doing so she not only fooled others, but—even more importantly—she fooled herself as well.

Remember: PMA is important! Fake it until you make it!

Study questions

1. Who said, "Although I disagree with what you say, I will defend to the death your right to say it."?
2. What is speechfright?
3. What is the psychological concept of flight or fight?
4. Is speechfright a normal response? Explain.
5. What speechfright symptoms do you exhibit? List at least three.

Works Cited in Chapter

Bruskin Associates. "What Are Americans Afraid Of?" *The Bruskin Report, 53* (July 1973).

Jeffers, Susan. *Feel the Fear and Do It Anyway.* New York: Fawcett Columbine, 1987.

Roper-Starch. "How Americans Communicate." National Communication Association, 1998. 22 May 2002 <http://www.natcom.org/research/Poll/how_americans_communicate.htm>.

Ethics in Communication

Throughout life, and particularly in the business world, we frequently have to make decisions that require ethical judgments. Decisions have to be made about with whom and how to live, what life occupation to pursue, how to value material possessions, and how to make ethical decisions.

For purposes of this discussion, we will define ethics as the standards you use for making decisions about how to behave. An ethical decision, therefore, is a decision based on your individual beliefs.

On the job you make decisions on whether to speak accurately or misleadingly, on how and what to report on your expense account, on how you use your on-the-job power or authority. You may have never consciously *examined* the standards on which you base those decisions, but you have them nonetheless.

Similarly, we all struggle with ethical concerns about how to set our goals and how to solve problems in ways that reflect our standards. The decisions a speaker makes about what information or arguments to convey to an audience reflect his or her character.

Values and Ethics Relate

Although a lot of people use the terms "values" and "ethics" as virtual synonyms, and they do relate to each other, they are not the same thing. When we talk about your values, we simply refer to whatever you believe is important. Naturally, your ethics are based on your values.

For example, Bill may consider it very important to always tell the truth. In other words, he values truth for its own sake. This leads to an ethical standard for Bill as a speaker: he will not knowingly lie to an audience. Susan may consider it important to be consistent in what she tells an audience because she knows that if audience members catch her in a lie, they will reject what she says and become angry with her. She values not angering the audience. Therefore she sets an ethical standard for herself: she will not knowingly lie to an audience.

> **We may label someone else as having no ethics, whereas in fact all have ethics because all have rules.**

You can see that Bill and Susan have similar ethics, but they are based on different values. We might call Bill's value altruistic and Susan's self-serving—but that is, itself, a judgment rather than an observation.

Another way to think of it is that your ethics can be observed based on your behavior. Your values are not necessarily so clear.

We Are the Product of Our Environments

Each of us carries baggage with us. This baggage includes our own personal biases we have about religion, race, sex, finance, and politics. This baggage also includes our attitudes about ethics. We may label someone else as having no ethics, whereas in fact all have ethics because all have rules. It's more useful to recognize the other person has *different* ethical standards—in other words, don't assume an "ethical person" will automatically do what you do. Almost everyone considers himself to be ethical, simply because he usually follows his own rules.

Ethics as a Process

We acquire habits, attitudes, and ethical beliefs throughout life based on our experiences and what we are taught. Individual ethical beliefs, then, reflect the result of individual experiences and learning. This individualized process leads each human being to form her ethical standards or "ethics."

Ethical Rightness

We influence and are influenced by environments relevant to our speaking. Anticipated reactions and known attitudes of others and critics influence each decision we make. From most ethical perspectives any organization or speaker that knowingly distributes harmful products, pollutes the environment, engages in deceptive advertising, or mistreats its employees should be criticized. The actual judgment we make regarding decisions in business and industry depend on the particular ethical baggage and beliefs we have accumulated.

Every day we must decide how to conduct ourselves ethically. Consider the following examples:

1. A doctor must choose whether or not to prescribe a placebo (harmless drug) for a patient whose illness is only in the mind (hypochondria).
2. An insurance salesman must decide how to convince an elderly couple to purchase homeowner's insurance (whether they need it or not).
3. A speaker/business person wrestles with the ethical decision of whether to present the oral presentation as the research or findings indicate, or to report the data falsely or inaccurately to support a selling point.

4. A business man or woman wrestles with the ethical decision of whether or not to report employee misconduct.

The above examples involve deciding right or wrong, good or bad, fair or unfair—decisions of ethical significance. Our personal ethical responsibilities are an important consideration in ethical correctness.

In a society where right or wrong sometimes falls into a gray area, it becomes increasingly hard to make the correct ethical decisions. In view of the complexity of today's society, it behooves all who struggle with ethical correctness to follow the golden rule: "Do unto others as you have them do unto you."

Being ethically correct is the speaker's prime responsibility.

While it is true that different people follow different ethical standards, it is also true that research suggests a set of ethical standards that serve a speaker well. Following these standards generally helps you as a speaker, even if your personal values would allow you to violate them in some way, simply because we assume that, as a speaker, you want the audience to accept and act on what you tell them.

For instance, you may have no qualms whatsoever about lying to an audience when you believe it is "for their own good." Even if you feel that way, it's still not a good idea to lie to the audience because the first item on the list shows that the audience tends to reject your ideas if they find out you've lied to them. They don't care if you think you have a good reason. They still reject your ideas.

Here, then, is a set of suggested ethical guidelines for speakers that represents a compilation of several studies:

1. *Lying is unethical.* Of all the attitudes about ethics, this is the one most universally held. When people

know they are being lied to, they will usually reject the speaker's ideas; if they find out later they were lied to, they often look for ways to punish the speaker who lied to them. As in most things dealing with public speaking, all communication is audience-centered. You may be absolutely truthful with them, but if you are perceived as lying, they will still reject what you have to say. You must sound sincere as well as be sincere. It also doesn't matter whether you can justify something to yourself as having not really been a lie. If they see it that way, they will treat it that way.

2.   *Name-calling is unethical.* Again, there seems to be an almost universal agreement on this guideline. Even though many people call others names in their interpersonal communication, they say they regard name-calling by public speakers to be unethical. The emphasis here is on the phrase "by public speakers." They may see it as fine in private, but unacceptable in public. Once again, the key is whether they see it as name-calling. The fact that politicians engage in this regularly does not disprove the contention; in fact, the general public attitude toward politicians demonstrates it. Politicians' habits simply show the strength of the temptation. Avoid it.

3.   *Grossly exaggerating or distorting facts is unethical.* Although some people seem willing to accept a little exaggeration as an element of human nature, most people consider "gross" or "distorted" exaggeration to be equivalent to lying. Because the line between some exaggeration and gross exaggeration or distortion often is difficult to distinguish, many people see any exaggeration as unethical. The trick

here, as always, is to keep your communication "audience-centered." Figuring out what a particular audience will see as exaggeration can be quite difficult. From the standpoint of credibility, you're better off to understate rather than overstate. When the audience members realize that such is your habit, it tends to give anything you say more weight. Exaggeration for the sake of humor is also more acceptable; just be certain it is perceived that way. This one is obviously related to number 1 above.

4. *Condemning people or ideas without divulging the source of the information is unethical.* Where ideas originate often matters as much as the ideas themselves. Although a statement may be true regardless of its source, people want more than the speaker's word for any damning statement. If you are going to discuss the wrongdoing of a person or the stupidity of an idea by relying on the words or ideas of others, you must be prepared to share the sources of those words or opinions. This standard relates to number 2 above. Logically, where information originates doesn't affect whether it is true. But people are not logical; they are psychological. The source affects whether people accept the information. To illustrate: there seems to be a perception that newspapers use a lot of stories attributed to anonymous sources. In fact, counting the number of such stories in a given issue of a newspaper and comparing it to the total number shows such stories really seldom run. Often there is not a single such story in an issue. But because its usage jars the consciousness so much, it sticks out in people's memories, thus making it seem more common than it is (like your consciousness of red

lights vs. green lights in traffic). People want to know sources for anything damaging, and will often reject information they would otherwise have accepted when it doesn't have a source.

5. *Suppression of key information is unethical.* If you have material to support your views, you should present it; if you have a motive that affects your view, you should divulge it. Audience members have the right to make a choice, but they must have full information in order to exercise that right. Again, the perception is the key. If, for instance, you are lobbying in a county commission meeting for the county to build a shopping center in a certain location, and you own property that will rise in value as a result, it is better to point this out up front. This allows you to say, "Yes, I will benefit, but I would favor this even if I didn't personally benefit because...." If your personal benefit is disclosed later, it can lead audience members to discount all the *other* reasons you gave. Even if you have nothing to hide, failure to disclose something that *they* think you should have can lead them to *believe* you have something to hide.

> **Even if you have nothing to hide, failure to disclose something that *they* think you should have can lead them to *believe* you have something to hide.**

You will have many more decisions to make, of course, but these guidelines give a solid basis for making sure your audience members hear, accept, and act on your ideas.

Study questions
1. What is the difference between ethics and values?
2. Why is "being ethically correct the speaker's prime responsibility"?
3. What are the five guidelines for speaker ethics?
4. Why are the five guidelines useful for a speaker regardless of the speaker's individual values?

Chapter 5

Audience Analysis

Speechmaking centers around the audience. Your primary reason for speaking is not showing off or gratifying yourself, but rather getting a desired response from your audience. That's why we say all communication is *audience-centered*.

That doesn't mean that you say just anything to get the response you want. Nor does it mean you have to change your beliefs to match the audience's. It does mean you have to take them into account every step of the way.

> **Your primary reason for speaking is not showing off or gratifying yourself, but rather getting a desired response from your audience.**

For instance, if you want to do a speech on a technical topic such as nuclear reactors, you will speak quite differently when speaking to a group of nuclear scientists than when talking to a group of fifth-graders. The focus will certainly differ (the scientists will not be interested in "How Reactors Work"; neither will the fifth-graders be interested in "Latest Advances in Breeder Reactor Technology"). The language will differ. The examples will differ.

On another level, your approach will differ depending on whether the audience is supportive or not.

So it is essential to understand the people you're talking to. The entire time you're working on your speech, keep several questions in mind:

☐ To whom am I speaking?

☐ What do I want them to know, believe, or do as a result of my speech?

☐ What is the most effective way of composing and presenting my speech to accomplish that aim?

You are more likely to connect with your audience when you have some understanding of three overarching factors about the audience and their relationship to your topic:

- The audience's attitude toward your topic.
- The audience's interest in your topic.
- The audience's knowledge of your topic.

You have to think about all three of these, because none of them bear any necessary relationship to the other two. For instance, they may have a great deal of knowledge about your topic but have very little interest in it, or a negative attitude toward it.

So let's examine some ways of getting at those three factors.

Demographics

Understanding the demographic factors can give you an indication about the three overarching factors. However, you have to be careful with this process, since you really are making an educated guess. If the average age of the audience is 55, it's a pretty good guess they don't know much about hip-hop music. It's not *certain*, however, and if you assume it is you may be surprised. The best way to use demographics is to make an educated guess based on them and then *check your guess* some other way.

Here are some of the most common demographic factors:

√ *Age.*

√ *Gender.* Be wary about making assumptions. Avoid sexist language.

√ *Racial, ethnic, or cultural background.*

√ *Religion.* Again, be wary about making assumptions.

√ *Group membership and affiliation.*

Situational Analysis

These are audience traits unique to the situation in which you will speak. They include:

√ *Size.* The larger your audience, the more formal your presentation should be.

√ *Physical setting.* Which would you prefer, an audience crammed into a classroom with too few and uncomfortable desks in August with the air conditioning broken, or one seated in cushioned seats in air-conditioned comfort in a well-lighted, airy room? Ask plenty of questions about the physical setting. Change what you can and adapt to what you can't to provide the best experience for the audience.

√ *Disposition toward speaker.*

√ *Disposition toward the occasion.* Telling jokes to start the speech may or may not be a good practice (we'll talk more about that in another article). Doing so to start off a funeral oration may be considered in very poor taste. Another factor is the time element. Figure out now how long your speech should be. Keep your speech within that time limit no matter what.

Gathering the Information

So how do you get all this information? Here are some practical ways:

Observation and Conversation

If you will speak to a group to which you belong (such as a class, a workgroup, or a club), pay attention with fresh eyes in the meetings prior to your speech. Get to know the people in an interpersonal way; you'll be able to work into your speeches the things you learn.

Interviews

This can be a time-consuming but useful approach, and you can implement it in several ways. Call audience members on the telephone beforehand to ask them some questions, or take one or more to lunch. Recognize that one person may or may not be representative of the group, so try to interview more than one.

Question the Person Who Contacted You

Interview the person who asked you to speak—similar to the last point, but a special case since this is the person who actually invited you to speak. Take into account that s/he may give you the group's viewpoint, or may just give you his/her own viewpoint. Consider asking questions that will give you an accurate picture regardless of the responses the contact gives.

> **She may give you the group's viewpoint, or may just give you his/her own viewpoint.**

To point out the approach: Most people, if asked, will claim to be unprejudiced. One of the authors had a relative who once said in response to such a question, "No, of course I'm not prejudiced. Those people [she named a specific group] can't help it if they're not as smart as white people. That's not prejudice, that's just fact." She exemplified the way a lot of people think. They're giving you an honest answer from their point of view, but it may not be accurate for your purposes. In such a case, get a more accurate picture by asking questions that surround the issue, like, "What would you do if one of your children dated someone of a different race?" or "Have you ever had a non-white boss? What did you do?" or "How many friends do you have who come from a different race than your own?" These are more objective questions that get behind the bigger question, and it also helps you avoid arguing with the other person about whether they're prejudiced or not.

So instead of asking about a group's political stance, for instance, you could ask who the last five speakers have been, what did they talk about, how did the audience react, etc.

Questionnaires

Textbooks really like this one, but you seldom get an opportunity to pass out questionnaires to audience members in real life. If you get the chance to do so, take advantage of it.

There are three basic types of questions for questionnaires:

Fixed-alternative questions. These are like multiple-choice tests. The respondent is limited to what you offer by way of answers. For example:

Do you know anyone involved in homeschooling?
yes_____ no_____ not sure_____

Scale questions. Although you still limit the respondents, they have more leeway. For example:

Do you agree or disagree with this statement: Homeschooling is an educationally superior alternative to public or private corporate schooling. Check the appropriate response.

Strongly agree   Agree   Undecided   Disagree
Strongly disagree

Open-ended questions. These give maximum leeway in responding. They also increase the likelihood of getting off-target answers. They look like this:

Under what circumstances do you believe homeschooling should be allowed?

Because each type of question has advantages and disadvantages, most quetionnaires use a mix of question types.

In summary, then, do everything you can to learn about your audience members before you speak to them. Your "bottom line" is always to get your point across. You'll hit your target more often when you take the time to figure out where it is.

Study questions
1. What does "audience-centered" mean?
2. What are demographics?
3. How are demographics useful to a speaker?
4. What are some useful techniques for gathering information about an audience?

Chapter 6

Choosing Purposes and Topics

Before you start working on your speech, decide why you are giving it (just because the teacher assigns it is not a good reason!). Deciding on the general purpose for speaking helps you focus on the type of topic and/or thesis you want to explore in your speech. The purpose gives the topic direction and determines the type of speech you make.

First of all, think about your audience members. Do you want them to agree with you, to be entertained by you, to understand the message you present, or to learn how to perform a task because of what you are teaching them?

You may have responded to the question in the past paragraph by saying, "Yes, I want my speech to be instructive, persuasive, and demonstrative—and I also want it to be entertaining!" If that was your answer then think through the issue again.

First decide on the focus of your speech; that focus is dependant on your purpose for speaking. While a speech may be entertaining as well as instructive or may persuade while it informs, **a speech should have one overriding, or primary, purpose.**

You must understand the primary response you want—and can realistically achieve—from your audience. Having more than one primary purpose often waters down the thesis because of the split focus on the topic.

> **The purpose gives the topic direction and determines the type of speech you make.**

As long as a speaker is sure of his primary purpose, he may then include secondary information that can contain other reasons for speaking. A persuasive speech should be as entertaining as possible—you want your audience to stay interested in what you say. An instructive speech on cigarette smoking may have a general purpose to inform, but if the information actuates someone to quit smoking, then the speech has served another purpose.

The general purposes for extemporaneous public speaking are divided into categories: instruction, persuasion, and special purposes. These categories may further be divided into groupings discussed below.

Instructive Speeches

- to inform
- to demonstrate
- to explain a value
- to entertain (this may also be considered a general category)

The instructive speech is given to share knowledge: "I know something that you ought to know, and I'm going to tell it to you." The speech may be informative; it may include statements of personal value; or it may be designed to teach or demonstrate.

In general, if you choose to instruct you are presenting information that you believe your audience should know. The information may or may not be of a controversial nature (the more controversial the topic, the more potentially interesting the speech). Remember, if the topic *is* controversial and your purpose is to inform, then don't fall into the trap of trying to explain the argument to the audience and obviously trying to get the audience to agree with you at the same time. Your explanation about the nature of the controversy may be all the information the audience can handle at one time.

The Informative Speech. The simple informative speech is a speech to give or share knowledge. It may consist of background, new information, and a supported opinion or two.

The biggest problem with informative speeches is that they may lack built-in audience interest. You have to work much harder to get and to keep your audience's attention and to convince the listeners that the information is important to each of them.

The Demonstration Speech. Often a speaker wants to teach his audience how to perform or complete a certain task. This type of speech is obviously important and fulfills a large need for the audience. Much popular television is demonstration oriented: Cooking shows and "how-to" shows, The Learning Channel, Discovery Channel, FOODTV, HGTV, and DIY are all "teaching through doing" vehicles.

The priority in a demonstration speech is planning. You must carefully think through the speech and its demonstration, making sure you obtain and can operate the necessary equipment—that you have a clear, process-oriented outline. **The demonstration speech not only shows how to do something; it tells why the process is performed a certain way.**

The Values Speech. Often a speaker needs to explain to the audience why she feels or believes a certain way. In other words, she must define her values to the audience. This purpose differs from persuasion in that it is simply to explain what ideas the speaker believes matter, rather than to convince the audience to agree with the speaker. The value may be as weighty as a belief in a certain religion or as narrow as explaining why an old beat-up toy has sentimental value.

A values speech may in effect be more persuasive than a simple informative speech. As Aristotle said, "All rhetoric is persuasive." But it is worthwhile to think of the values speech as informative—or at least "pre-persuasive." To persuade audience members, you must go beyond more information and appeal to their values, i.e., to what they consider important. However, simply explaining values is no more persuasive necessarily than explaining other kinds of information. To persuade, you must ask your audience to agree with you or to do something as a result of your speech.

A values speech gives you an opportunity (but not a license) to preach. This is your opportunity to get on your soapbox. Values speaking allows you to assert your own personal point of view, but it can also address the opposition's point of view or fears. A values speech will offer an open-minded approach, thus allowing the audience members to feel that the decision is theirs, rather than "ramming the thesis statement down their throats."

The Speech to Entertain. We often think of entertainment speeches as after-dinner speeches because that is when we hear them the most. After a person has eaten a full meal, he is not usually in the mood to listen to a debate or an intense intellectual discourse; he wants to relax and be entertained. A speaker may sneak in an important thought or two in an after dinner speech, but not much more.

Don't assume that examining this category separately means you should avoid entertainment in other types of speeches. All speeches should strive to be entertaining, because humor and pathos help hold and win an audience. Rarely is the primary purpose of a speech *just* to entertain. When it is, don't lose sight of that purpose. When your purpose is to, for example, persuade, don't lose sight of that purpose at the expense of being entertaining.

Persuasive Speeches

- to make inroads into opinion
- to convince
- to actuate

> **A good persuasive speaker must first understand the audience's position on the issue before she plans her specific purpose.**

The ultimate goal of persuasion is to get others to take action on the speaker's thesis. A wise speaker knows that such commitment is not always possible in one speech. Selling an idea or a product takes time, and the sales technique must be planned. A good persuasive speaker must first understand the audience's position on the issue before she plans her specific purpose. She must understand her **audience demographics,** those characteristics of each audience that strongly influence opinion (see Chapter 5 for more detail on audience analysis).

When a speaker speaks to persuade, he tries to get audience members to open their minds to his ideas, to agree with him, or to act upon a previous agreement. In general, persuasion is the attempt to change or reinforce an attitude, belief, or behavior. A speaker, then, has to pick one of the three different specific purposes in order to persuade his audience.

An In-Roads Speech. If the speaker feels that the audience members (or a majority of them) will never agree with him, then he designs his persuasive speech to get

51

them to listen with an open mind rather than form a new opinion. The speaker makes **inroads into their opinions.**

A Speech to Convince. If the speaker wants to change audience members' minds or help them develop an opinion where none exists, then she presents the information in a positive and reasonable manner to her audience; this is called **convincing,** or **simple persuasion.** It is based on the belief that the audience demographic demonstrates a soft opinion or no opinion of the topic.

A Speech to Actuate. If a speaker believes that the audience members are already inclined to agree with him, he may then attempt to lead them into action, to have them put their physical commitments where their attitudes are. This form of persuasion is called **actuation.**

Because persuasion is such an important part of learning to speak extemporaneously, the finer points of persuasion will be explained in Chapter 15.

Other General Purposes for Speaking

Special Occasion Speeches

Wedding toasts, eulogies, sermons, testimonials—all are other common types of speaking. Many of these purposes do not require the same amount or type of research as the more traditional extemporaneous speech, but all follow the basic organizational concept of planning, organization, and delivery. Even short speeches require planning to be effective.

Specific Purpose

What, specifically, do you want your audience to gain from your speech?

**At the end of my speech I want my audience
to_____.** When you fill in this blank, you know the
audience outcome you seek from your speech. That is your
specific purpose. The infinitive verb (to _____) must
match your general purpose. In other words, if your general purpose is instructive, then the verb should be "to
understand," " to know," " to appreciate," "to feel," or
similar verbs expressing the end effect on your audience.
Likewise, if your general purpose is to actuate, then your
infinitive verb should be "to do," "to buy," "to vote," or
some other action verb.

**Make sure your general purpose and your audience
outcome match in style and tone. Make sure your thesis
sentence reflects the tone of your purposes.**

Choosing a Topic

You may have spent an educational lifetime writing
papers or giving reports on topics someone else has assigned to you. In a way, this is good training—in the
business world you often have to speak about things that
other people want you to address. Nevertheless, you
almost always have to bring your own focus to the topic,
and often you have a lot of leeway within certain parameters for choosing a topic.

For many students, it is a welcome breath of freedom
to be able to choose your own topic. For others, it can be
very frightening, to the point of causing a sort of "writer's
block" before you have even begun writing a speech! Too
many who experience this find themselves involved in a
deadly sort of procrastination, stewing for so long over
which topic to choose that they wind up still choosing the
night before a speech is due, leaving *no* time for research,
rehearsal, organization, etc.

Therefore, we want to give you some tips and techniques for choosing a topic that fits the audience, the occasion and the speaker (that's you).

Who's in Charge Here?

Some students draw the conclusion that, since the teacher doesn't assign the topic, the speaker can talk about anything she wants to. But that's not true either. While the speaker must choose the topic, if you're going to be effective you must take several things into account other than *only* what you want to talk about.

The Top Two Considerations

Arguably **your own interests should be the *top* consideration**, just not the only one. This is true for a number of reasons—three should suffice to illustrate this.

> ## You must take several things into account other than *only* what you want to talk about.

1. *Start with your own interests because it makes your research more efficient.* One of the authors trained as a newspaper reporter. He would be able to research and talk about an unfamiliar topic, but it would take him much longer to find even basic information than it would take someone who was really "into" the topic. For instance, it would take me two days to gather the information on privately-fund ventures into space that a colleague of mine could gather in ten minutes, simply because she already has all the information. What's more, she is on a first-name basis with people in that area, and thus has easy, quick access to the latest information that hasn't even been published yet. If she talked on that topic, she could take the time saved in research and apply it to organizing and rehearsing the speech.

2. *Start with your own interests because it makes your enthusiasm natural.* Enthusiasm is difficult to fake. Why should you have to? Just choose something for which you have natural enthusiasm. It is relatively harder to take something you think an audience cares about and develop enthusiasm about it than it is to infect them with your own enthusiasm. They may have not even been very interested to begin with, but may become so out of sheer curiosity for what it is that has obviously engaged *you*.

3. *Start with your own interests because it makes dealing with stage fright easier.* One of the techniques we discuss in Chapter 3 for dealing with communication anxiety hinges on the "green monkey principle." That principle basically says that you can only focus on one thing at a time. If you want to stop thinking about a green monkey, think about a pink elephant instead. If you want to stop thinking about your fear, think about your topic instead. That is much easier to do if you have picked a topic you care about.

But you can't *only* think about your interests. **Your second major consideration** should be **tying your interests to your audience's interests**. Unless you tell them in some way why your topic matters to *them*, they will have no reason to listen.

One summer a salesman came to the front door of one of the authors. As he tells it:

> *The salesman said, "If you'll just buy a subscription to this magazine, I can win a trip to Hawaii." I was already hot and tired, and this approach did nothing to improve my mood. I said, "Why should I care if you go to Hawaii? I just want you off my door step." And I shut the door.*

He would have had a lot more luck holding my attention and even making the sale if he had just asked a few questions and looked at his offering from my *point of view. I'm sure HIS reason for selling magazines was to win a trip or make money, but those are not my reasons for buying. He would have satisfied his wants by understanding MY reasons for buying and then appealing to them.*

So why should the audience want to listen to you? One of us once knew another student in graduate school who was truly enthusiastic about accounting, but recognized that other people did not find double-entry book-keeping as fascinating. However, when he asked something like, "How would you like to save $500 on your taxes?" he got other people's attention (and held it as long as he talked in their language instead of accounting jargon). He started with his interests, and quickly tied it to the audience's interests.

Sometimes it's just a matter of seeing your topic from the audience's viewpoint. A topic that may have become mundane to you because of your familiarity with it may be exciting to someone else because it seems exotic. Even astronauts can reach a point in which their work becomes "just my job five days a week," as in Elton John's song *Rocket Man* (lyrics by Bernie Taupin).

Other Considerations

In addition to the above major considerations, other things to consider include:

√ What's physical environment for the speech? (Indoors/ outdoors, audience seated or standing, type of speaking space.)

√ What's the speaking environment? (Length of speech,

demographics of the audience, etc.)
√ How much preparation time do I have?

Things That Don't Really Matter

We can also see several common missteps in choosing a topic. For instance, people often worry about finding enough material. But in the "information age," the problem usually isn't finding *enough* material, but rather finding an appropriate *filter* for the material. You will find much more than you need on almost any topic.

Compare, for instance, a typical 10-page report for a class with a five-minute speech. The 10-page report, on average, will comprise about 2,500 words. The typical five-minute speech (given an average speaking rate in the United State of 120 to 150 words per minute) would comprise only 750 words. Yet beginning speakers often try to do enough research on a topic for a small book, and then attempt to cram all of it into the allotted five minutes. The result tends to be shallow and boring.

It also matters little what is on the cover of *Time* or *Newsweek* this week, unless it happens to be something that matters to you personally. If it truly matters to you, go ahead and talk about it. But remember that if it's really a hot topic, everyone else has read the same sources you have. They've seen the same TV shows. If you are to keep them engaged and not waste their time, find something unique that *you* can bring to the topic.

This is not to say your sources don't matter. They do—they matter a great deal, in fact. But it is your unique approach, your handling of the material, that makes it a speech rather than simply reporting on what they could just as easily have found for themselves.

What If I'm Still Stuck?

You probably need to break the process down into steps. Most people have problems at this stage because they're trying to narrow their choices down from a thousand possibilities to one topic in one step.

First build up your raw material. Jot down every topic you can think of in which you would have some interest. Don't stop to judge it, just jot it down. You can decide to leave it out later. (You may recognize the basic pattern of "brainstorming" here. All we're doing is using brainstorming to generate a topic.)

If you have trouble getting started on *that* list, start by coming up with very general categories, such as people, places, hobbies, issues, etc. Then list everything you can think of under the general headings.

From this list, pick the top 10. Narrow it down to five based on your own interests. At that point, think in

Sample Topics

Just to get you started, here are some sample topics for extemporaneous speaking. It is designed to spark your imagination so that you can pick topics that you are comfortable with. Don't just choose one from this list. However, something here may serve as a seed. For instance, the "Local Elections" topic under "Political Topics" may make you think about voting rights in other countries, which makes you think about a recent election in which the incumbent used the army to intimidate voters, which makes you think about the United Nations "observing" elections, which leads you to talk about whether the United States should be involved in monitoring elections in other countries.

Remember, just about any topic is acceptable as long

as it is researchable and appropriate for the audience. Your teacher may give you guidelines as to which specific topics you may or may not use.

Political Topics
The New Russia
Israel: Today and Tomorrow
State's Rights vs. Federalism
Sunni and Shiite Muslims
Life in a Medieval Castle
The Importance of Pearl Harbor
Presidential Debates
The Dead Sea Scrolls
A Peaceful Outer Space
Star Wars
Local Elections
Should a School Superintendent Be Elected?
Local Liquor Laws
Taxes, Taxes, Taxes
Pornography in Today's Society
Lotteries
Consolidated Government
Equal Rights for All
Opinion Polls
The Electoral College
The Power of the Supreme Court

Should TVA Be Privatized?
Universal Health Insurance
How Should We Be Taxed?
Private Clubs and Discrimination
Congressional Redistricting
Should Churches Be Taxed?
Censorship
A Government Run by Seniority
Is the Solid South Still Solid?
The "New" China
The Global Role of the USA in the New Century
The New United States of Europe
Is NATO Obsolete?
The World: Six Billion and Counting
The US Role in Latin America
Freedom

Global Terrorism
The Global Village
Global Trouble Spots
How Should Cable TV
Be Regulated
Nuclear Disarmament
The Future of the UN
Japan: Economic Friend
or Foe?
Dictators
US-Friendly Dictators
Our Fifty-first State
European Balance of
Power
Amending the Constitu-
tion
State Sales Tax
State Income Tax
"All Men Are Created
Equal"
Personal Liberty
The Right of Free Speech
Morality
Ethics
Evolution vs. Divine
Creation
"A Woman's Place Is in
the Home"
Movies Made from
Novels
Why Study Science?
World Population: 2010
AD
Raising the Minimum
Wage

Competition with Japan
and Others
What Happened to the
Metric System?
The Greenhouse Effect
Are Foreign Cars Better?
African Poachers
Censorship and the
Internet

Education
Student Activities Fees
Free Press and a School
Newspaper
The Obligation Not to
Cheat
The Role of Athletics on
the College Campus
Are College Sports
Professional?
Financial Aid for Stu-
dents
Day Care on College
Campuses
A Valuable College
Course
Fraternities: Good or Bad
Are Community College
Students Cheating
Their Social Life?
The Role of Student
Government
The Handicapped and
Higher Education

Should Teachers Teach
the Student or the
Course?
The Grading System, Pro
and Con
Should Physical Educa-
tion Be Required?
Valid Higher Education:
Culture vs. Career
Academic Freedom
How Do We Evaluate
Our Educational
System?
The Value of Higher
Education
Liberal Arts vs. Technol-
ogy
Should Student Athletes
Be Paid?
What Is a Relevant
Curriculum?
All Students Should Be
Required to Take a
Foreign Language
A New Curriculum for a
New Century
What Makes a Great
Teacher?
Them That Can, Do;
Them That Can't,
Teach.
Extending the School
Year

Law and Crime
The Fairness of a Trial by
Jury
Mandatory Lie Detector
Tests for Jobs
Mandatory Drug Tests
for Jobs
White Collar Crime
The Perfect Crime
Must We Give Up Our
Rights to Combat
Crime?
Electronic Fingerprints
Should Capital Punish-
ment Be Abolished?
Sexual Harassment
The Cost of Crime
Should the Elderly Lose
Their Drivers' Li-
censes?
Assault Rifles

Today and Tomorrow
High Tech, Today and
Tomorrow
What Will the New
Century Bring?
My Greatest Future Fear
My Greatest Future Hope
Raising the Minimum
Wage
Competition with Japan
and Others

Nuclear Energy: Worth
  the Risk?
Acid Rain
Fission vs. Fusion
Water Pollution
Malls, Malls, Malls
The Selling of a Politi-
  cian
Cable TV of the Future
How Safe Is Air Travel?
America and Its Love of
  the Automobile
New Methods of Surgery
The Biggest Problems of
  the Biggest Cities
The Homeless
Space and Beyond
Is the Shuttle System
  Worth It?
A New Superhighway
  System
Can They Cure the
  Common Cold?
What Do We Know
  about the Weather?
The Greenhouse Effect
The Newest Diet
Are We Living Longer?
Are We Living Better?
The World Our Grand-
  children Will Know
Tornadoes
How To Use Natural
  Predators To Eat/Kill
  Mosquitos

Home and Family
How Best to Use Our
  Leisure Time
Parent-Child Relation-
  ships
The Nuclear Family
Living Alone
The Need to Reproduce
Career vs. Family
Should Homosexuals
  Adopt?
Exercise for Life
A Proper Diet
Budgeting in the Home
Home Businesses
Stress and the Single
  Parent
Latch-key Kids

Study questions
1. What are the purposes of informative speaking?
2. What are the purposes of persuasive speaking?
3. What is the difference between an extemporaneous speech and an impromptu speech?
4. What are the strengths and weaknesses of each type of public speaking?

Chapter 7

Researching Your Speeches

Audiences generally expect you to know what you're talking about. As we point out in our discussion of ethos, logos, and pathos, one of your most potent tools in your toolbox is your credibility as a speaker. You can lose your credibility easily, and find it very hard to win back. For that reason, as well as others, you owe it to yourself and your audience to find the best information you can, and verify it to the best of your ability. You also should cite your sources to your audience members, so they *know* that you have "done your homework," and so they can follow up on your information if they wish.

> **You can lose your credibility easily, and find it very hard to win back.**

We won't go through the kind of basic "how to find information" material you likely learned in high school and also learned more deeply in a college English composition class. Our focus will be on using these sources in the special way required by oral communication, and avoiding the special problems.

Personal Experience

Your personal experience shows up more often in speeches than in formal papers and business research—and it should. Your personal experience helps the audience a great deal, especially for interpreting other information in your speech. Personal experience can be an excellent form of soft supporting material (see Chapter 10).

Bear a couple of warnings in mind, however.

Avoid the Extremes

Speakers tend to go to the extremes of including *no* personal information or experience (so the "speech" becomes a research report) or including *only* personal information or experience (so the "speech" becomes an oral editorial). When you present *only* your personal experience, audiences find it easy to dismiss it as not representative of general experience—"it's just your opinion." Leaving it out, though, makes it hard for audience members to relate to the research you present.

Verify Your Experience/knowledge

A lot of people "know" things that turn out to be untrue. Since you're human, you're probably not an exception. If you have factual information running around in your head, you learned it somewhere. Try to remember where, or at least try to find similar information. (Search engines on the World Wide Web can make this easier than ever.) Such a process will also help you determine the gaps in your knowledge and help you plan your other research.

Distinguish Opinion from Knowledge

It's not bad to have an opinion, but make sure you know the difference between factual information (which forms the basis of opinion) and the opinions you have about information.

For instance, if the mechanics told you the repair to your car would cost $200, and they charge you $500 when you pick it up, you may tell a friend that "the garage robbed me" and believe it to be factual. That is, in fact, your opinion. It may be a very accurate opinion. But if you mistake it for fact, you could have all kinds of problems, including legal ones.

Think in terms of what you can see, hear, smell, taste, and feel. "James got angry" may *sound* like an observation of fact, but it is actually a judgment. What did you actually see and hear? "James raised his voice, turned red in the face, and used language he doesn't usually use. From this I conclude that he became angry."

Using the Internet

You probably know far more than we do about surfing the 'Net. If you don't, find a 12-year-old to teach you. Our concern here is not so much "how to" but "what to beware."

Illustration by Todd Long

The problem with the Internet is that *anyone* can put up a Web page for little or no money. Someone who has thought about a subject for, say, five minutes can, with a little knowledge of Web design, make a page appear as slick and professional as a Web page published by someone who has actually done a lot of research and thinking about the topic. So how can you tell it's a reliable source?

Here are some guidelines that will help make your use of the Internet more reliable:

Is the Information Available Somewhere Else?

If you found the information via a search on *The Atlantic Monthly* Web site, it will usually refer you to the print edition in which the same article was published. Although not a guarantee, organizations that go to the trouble and expense of publishing the information in a magazine or book are more likely to check the information first—they have more at stake.

Evaluate the Source

- Is the author clearly identified?
- Does the author list her credentials?
- Can you check out the credentials?
- Does the author list professional affiliations?
- Does the author provide a means of contacting him (mail address, e-mail address, telephone number)?
- Does the e-mail address work? (Try sending an e-mail to the author—most won't mind. If it "bounces" (comes back as undeliverable), it's a bit suspicious. If someone else answers it, don't worry—having someone who "screens" your e-mail generally indicates the presence of an organization, which actually makes the information more reliable.)

Evaluate the Information Itself

- Does the Web page author include sources and attributions?
- How recent is the information (i.e., does the information itself come from recent sources)?
- How recently was the page updated?
- Are differing points of view presented?
- What is the quality of the writing? (Badly written material is not necessarily produced by an unreliable source, but it's a good indication. Brilliant thinkers who are bad writers usually hire good editors. Not doing so may indicate a simple crackpot.)

Interviewing Sources

Personal interviews can get you supporting material you can't get any other way. The information is immediate, personal, and often deals with cutting-edge material that hasn't had time to be published. It can be an excellent source of soft supporting material, as well as hard supporting material in the form of expert testimony (see Chapter 10).

Even when you hook up with a genuinely expert source, do your homework first.

Use caution, however. If you interview your brother-in-law about his opinion on cloning, and he works with you at the movie theater, it doesn't mean much. He's entitled to his opinion, and it may be a perfectly well-informed one, but it doesn't lend any weight to your speech. On the other hand, if your brother-in-law has read a lot on the subject you can get "referrals" to his sources and make them your own. Go find the information he read and use *that* as your source.

Even when you hook up with a genuinely expert source, do your homework first. If you have managed to get an interview with a scientist from Oak Ridge National Laboratories, don't waste her time asking her about things you could easily look up in basic textbooks, like, "What exactly is a breeder reactor?" Look it up first. Then you will be prepared to ask her about the latest development in breeder reactors, or how she got started working with them, or where she thinks the field will go next.

Here are some guidelines for conducting interviews[*]:

1. Stay with concrete, sense-oriented questions. When they give you a general or summary answer, probe for what's behind it. "He got angry." "What makes you think he was angry? What did he look like? What did he do? What did he say?"
2. See through their eyes, hear through their ears.

"Pretend I'm blind and I can only hear your voice. Now take me where you've been."

3. Don't jump to conclusions based on *your* experience. Pretend you're from Mars and you don't know at all what they're talking about. Get them to show you.

4. Magazine writers are told, "Show, don't tell." Get the material that will let you do that.

5. Start with non-threatening questions first. Develop the personal connection. But don't chitchat.

6. Don't just appear interested. Find a way to *be* interested.

7. Prepare your questions ahead of time.

8. Listen to the responses and ask new questions based on the responses—don't just slavishly follow your list.

9. Be willing to appear foolish.
    a. Ask naïve questions.
    b. Ask difficult questions.

10. Watch your body language. You can ask difficult, probing questions if your body language says you care and that you are interested. Feel the responses; don't just listen intellectually.

11. Your job is to draw them out, not to talk. Ask the questions, and then *listen*.

12. Look for patterns and themes in what they're saying. What comes up over and over?

13. Think about the relationship between "feelings" (as in "emotions") and feeling (as in one of the five senses). We experience emotions with our bodies. Go for that description.

14. Record the interview, but use the tape recorder only as backup.
    a. The recorder can't note the surroundings or

what your interviewee's expression looked like, etc.

    b.   The recorder can be adversely affected by background noise.

    c.   The battery can run down.

    d.   The tape can get eaten.

    e.   The tape recorder won't help you process what you're hearing.

15.   Take notes about everything.

    a.   Note surroundings, clothing, sounds, facial expressions, and gestures.

    b.   Write down quotations that give a flavor of verbal expression.

    c.   Use two columns: right-hand for notes, left-hand for notes about the notes (what strikes you, what could be a main point, etc.)

    d.   You can always leave it out later; if you don't write it down, it may be impossible to recapture.

Study questions

1.   What is the relationship between research and credibility?

2.   Why does it matter that you distinguish between opinion and fact?

3.   What are the strengths and weaknesses of using the Internet for research? What cautions should you follow?

Chapter 8

Principles of Organization

Outlining and organization are related, but they're not the same thing. Outlining is the *tool* by which we achieve organization. You can be organized without using an outline, and experience proves you can certainly have an outline without being organized.

Lots of resources show us how to outline—and those are valuable skills. A sample outline in the course will show you something about that. But look at it after you've read through this material, because you'll also be able to see the principles of organization in that sample outline.

Simplicity

Simplicity has lots of applications in the speaking process, but as we consider it in the context of organization, we mean to say this: The more complex your *message* the harder it will be for you to communicate it effectively.

> **The more complex your message the harder it will be for you to communicate it effectively.**

For this to make practical sense, remember that we differentiate between ideas and the message that represents those ideas. (See *What Is Communication* in Chapter 1 for a reminder.) *Ideas* may be complex, but we don't transfer ideas, we transfer symbols. So part of the challenge here is to find a simple way to symbolize or represent your ideas without slopping over into simplistic thinking.

The mass media are often accused of being simplistic, and there is some basis for this accusation.

Newspapers, for instance, typically write at a sixth or eighth grade level—not because readers can't read at a higher level, but because they don't want to. Think about your experience. You're perfectly capable of reading at a college level, but after you've done it all day, you don't want to go home and relax with a newspaper or magazine written at that level—it's too much work!

In pursuit of making the reading easy, then, newspa-

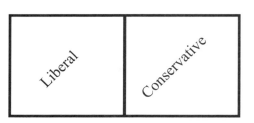

pers often go too far and damage the ideas they try to communicate to people. For instance, in politics the media can leave the impression that there are only two positions in politics: you're either liberal or conservative, as if everyone fit in a box:

It would be a little better if we used a spectrum instead of boxes—and they at least *try* to do that with labels such as "moderate Republican" or "conservative Democrat." At least that way, you could recognize that there are *degrees* of liberal and conservative.

The problem is that politics is much more complex than that. But we still need a simple way to represent political positions. Several years ago, someone came up with a grid to represent political positions. The grid is a simple device that gives a way to represent hundreds of political positions. To see how it works, take a look at the complete quiz at http://www.self-gov.org/wspq.html (or follow the link on the accompanying CD).

In the same way, we want to find simple ways to *represent* our ideas, without doing simplistic damage to the ideas.

You can achieve simplicity in several ways:

***To achieve simplicity of structure, be sure your specific purpose, thesis, and main points are very clear to* you.**

Take a look at Chapter 6 and make sure you know the difference between specific purpose and thesis. Within that context, here's a brief way of telling them apart: specific purpose is that which you want to accomplish. Your thesis is how you're going to go about accomplishing the specific purpose. For instance, in the military you might have an objective to "take the hill." There are dozens of ways you could go about doing that—send in paratroopers, bombard the hill, etc. But you have to *pick* one. If you tried to send in paratroopers **and** bombard the hill, you'd have a big problem.

Your specific objective might be: "To persuade my audience members to give blood during the Blue-Orange Blood Drive." (A UT student used that objective in a speech several years ago in a class one of us taught there. If you're not familiar with it, the University of Tennessee and the University of Kentucky compete each year to see who can raise the greatest number of donated pints of blood.) If your thesis is "You should give blood during the Blue-Orange Blood Drive to help UTK win," you will focus on the competition and may not even mention local blood needs. On the other hand, if your thesis is "You should give blood during the Blue-Orange Blood Drive to help your local community meet its blood needs," then you'll focus on blood shortages and the need to donate, and may not even mention the competitive aspects that would be central to the other speech. Either would be a good way to achieve the specific purpose.

Once you've established the specific purpose and the thesis, break the thesis down into a few main points (you'll see how many in the next section). These are the points you need to establish to explain or prove the thesis. Subpoints, in turn, will help you to explain or prove the main points. Everything winds up supporting the thesis, just as the struts in a bridge all combine to support the weight of the entire bridge.

A speech should have between two and five main points.

You've heard from English teachers that if you have a I. you have to have a II.; if you have an A., you have to have a B. The lower end of the range is probably not a new idea. The reason for the upper end of the range may be less clear, though.

If you're writing a book, you can put as many chapters in it as you want. When people read something, and don't quite get it, they can read back over it again. They can skim through it first to get a sense of the overall organization, then go back through a piece at a time. They can't do that with a speech.

We are limited by what people can retain and process in their short-term memories.

In effect, speakers are limited by what people can retain and process in their short-term memories.

You can retain huge amounts of complex information in *long*-term memory. But you have to move it there from *short*-term memory. The basic psychology text used at this college says that you can only retain about seven discrete items in short-term memory. "Discrete items" is determined psychologically. Discrete items may be the digits in a phone number, or seven concepts represented by seven sentences.

A key characteristic of short-term memory is that when it fills up, it doesn't act like a cup that retains what's already in there and simply cannot accept anymore. It acts more like a, well, like a toilet, in that it likely flushes everything.

The good news here is that since "discrete items" is a matter of perception, and since you control how things are grouped together, all you have to do is find or impose patterns on your information that make sense to your audience, and you will be able to get your speech into five main points or fewer. (See the example below.)

The main points should be phrased as simply as possible.
Simple here means a number of things:

- Only one sentence per point. If you have several sentences, you don't really have an outline; you have paragraphs that are broken up to look like an outline. If you think you need all those extra sentences, you need to break them out and make subpoint and sub-subpoints out of them.
- Use grammatically simple sentences (remember English comp?). Avoid compound, complex, and compound-complex construction. As above, simplify and make subpoint and sub-subpoints.
- Use psychologically simple sentences. In the first part of the example outline below, the sentences are technically simple sentences, but they don't *feel* simple. Compare to the structure of the second part of the example.

Symmetry

Symmetry means "proper balance." You might well ask, "If it means that, then (in keeping with the principle of simplicity) why not just call it that?" The reason is because of the principle of symmetry. This will become clearer when you understand the principle itself.

You display symmetry in your speeches in two main ways.

The timing of the speech.

If you have a five minute speech with three main points in which you spend four minutes on the introduction and the first main point, your speech is out of balance. The audience will not realize main points two and three are main points if you manage to squeeze the speech in under five minutes. If you balance them at this point, you will run fifteen minutes for a five-minute speech, which does not endear you to audiences.

Coherency (how the speech fits or flows together).

Here's how to achieve coherency:

√ Write the body first, to make sure intro and conclusion fit.

√ Make the introduction and conclusion relate to each other. If you wander off somewhere in the middle, you'll find it this way.

√ Follow a consistent pattern in developing the speech. This might be a consistent chronological pattern, geographic pattern (if you talk about four-year colleges in Tennessee, for instance, start in Memphis and consistently head east), or word pattern. We call this principle "symmetry" because that makes each principle start with the same sound, making it easier to remember the principles because there is a pattern.

Here's an example speech to show how these principles apply:

Thematic statement: Government welfare programs aren't working.

Main points:

I. We don't fund it sufficiently.

II. Some people who really need help are left out.

III. There are too many programs.

IV. The programs often duplicate coverage.

V. Money is wasted.

VI. The programs create dependence and stifle initiative.

VII. It robs the poor of self-respect.

VIII. Recipients have no input into what is really needed.

Contrast with:

Central idea: Our approach to welfare in America is inadequate, inefficient, and insensitive.

Main points:

I. Our approach is inadequate.

    A. We don't fund it sufficiently.

    B. Some people who really need help are left out.

II. Our approach is inefficient.

    A. There are too many programs.

    B. The programs often duplicate coverage.

    C. Money is wasted.

III. Our approach is insensitive.

    A. The programs create dependence and stifle initiative.

    B. It robs the poor of self-respect.

    C. Recipients have no input into what is really needed.

Study questions

1. What are the two primary principles of organization?

2. How are organization and outlining different? How are they related?

3. How can you achieve simplicity of organization?

<table>
<tr>
<td>

Chapter

9

</td>
<td>

Mechanics of Outlining

</td>
</tr>
</table>

Outlining and organization relate to each other, but they're not the same thing. You can organize your thoughts without using an outline, and lots of evidence indicate you can use an outline and not be organized. We've talked about the Principles of Organization in the last chapter. Now let's look at the process of constructing an outline.

Note: A useful step prior to constructing the outline involves mind-mapping. Material on that process can be found on the accompanying CD. You can use the following information without mind-mapping first, but it's easier *after* you have mind-mapped your topic.

What Is an Outline?

When people use the word *outline*, they may have different things in mind. A professional writer outlining a story may just use bulleted phrases. A speaker may bring brief notes to the lectern (for our purposes, we'll call that the "speaking outline"). A meeting chair may bring a list of items to be addressed. All of these are outlines. They're also all different from what *we* mean. To clarify what we mean, let's call ours a "preparation outline."

Calling it this helps us in at least a couple of ways. For one thing, it's a good reminder of something we've said several times: an outline is not an order of presentation, it's a map of the relationship of ideas. In other words, the preparation outline helps you to see how your thoughts relate to each other. The speaking outline may reorder the thoughts for the most effective presentation, but you still need to make sure the ideas relate properly. The distinction helps us see why we need a *full-sentence* outline. The sentence is the basic unit of logical thinking. When you have phrases, you may be headed toward complete thoughts, but you're not there yet. Once you've completed your full-sentence outline, you may then effectively reduce it to phrases as *reminders* of what you've thought about. This brings us to yet another benefit of the distinction: it helps you remember how *ineffective* it is to bring your full-sentence outline to the lectern with you.

> **Your preparation outline helps you to plan the relationship of ideas you want to present to your audience.**

So how should *this* outline look?

First, recognize each speech outline will have an *Introduction*, a *Body*, and a *Conclusion*. These parts should always be labeled. The labels do **not** get numbered.

Correct	Incorrect
Introduction	I. Introduction
Body	II. Body
Conclusion	III. Conclusion

Within each section, main points and subpoints will be numbered and indented according to standard outline conventions. It should look something like this:

Introduction		1.	Sub-subpoint
		2.	Sub-subpoint
I. Intro point		3.	Sub-subpoint
II. Intro point		B.	Subpoint
III. Intro point	III.	Main point	
		A.	Subpoint
Body		1.	Sub-subpoint
I. Main point		2.	Sub-subpoint
A. Subpoint		B.	Subpoint
B. Subpoint		1.	Sub-subpoint
1. Sub-subpoint		2.	Sub-subpoint
2. Sub-subpoint	Conclusion		
3. Sub-subpoint	I.	Conclusion point	
II. Main point	II.	Conclusion point	
A. Subpoint	III.	Conclusion point	

This isn't an ironclad, fill-in-the-blanks example. Your outline may have two main points, or four. A given subpoint may not have any sub-subpoints, or may have seven. The example just shows you how to mix main points, subpoints, and sub-subpoints.

How Do I Start?

You probably already have some idea what you want to talk about. Maybe you say, "I want to do a speech about organ donation." You don't have a topic yet—don't fool yourself. But you do have a good starting point. My question would be: "*What about* organ donation?" Go further. Develop your specific purpose and your central idea before doing anything else.

Specific purpose: At the end of my speech I want my audience members to sign up as organ donors.

Central idea: Everyone should become an organ donor in order to save lives.

The nature of specific purpose statements and central idea statements is discussed in Chapter 8. Check there if you need to, then come back here.

Your central idea or thesis is your "big idea." For your audience members to be able to follow you, understand the idea, and remember it, you'll have to break it up into bits they can handle. Your next step, then, is to take your thesis and break it up in a way that supports the thesis. (By "support" we mean "explain, illustrate, or prove.") When you do that, you'll have your main points (of the body of the speech). One way to do that is:

I.   There is a critical shortage of organ donors in this country.
II.   We can solve the shortage.

You start with your main points, which are sort of "divisions" of the thesis. Then you take each main point and divide it into subpoints. Where needed, you take a subpoint and divide it into sub-subpoints.

At the risk of offending vegetarians (which is *not* our intention), you approach building a speech the same way you approach eating a cow. The cow is too big to swallow whole. First you cut the cow up into steaks. Then you cut the steaks up into bite-sized pieces. I used to know someone who bought an entire cow at slaughtering time (back in the old days when most meat was not produced factory-style), had it butchered, then put in a large freezer. It fed him and his family for most of a year—one bite at a time.

You might divide our hypothetical speech this way, by taking each main point and dividing it further:

I.   There is a critical shortage of organ donors in this country.
      A.   40,000 people in the United States wait for transplants, according to *Health Index*.
      B.   Brigid McMenamin of *Health Index* says,

> "Last year 3,104 patients died waiting for a transplant."

    C.   Statistics from the University of Pittsburgh Medical Center put this into perspective.

    D.   Public misconceptions contribute to the lack of donors.

See how each of those help support the main point? As you look at those subpoints, you realize some of them need fleshing out also. Let's take it further.

I.   There is a critical shortage of organ donors in this country.

    A.   40,000 people in the United States wait for transplants, according to *Health Index*.

    B.   Brigid McMenamin of *Health Index* says, "Last year 3,104 patients died waiting for a transplant."

    C.   Statistics from the University of Pittsburgh Medical Center put this into perspective.

        1.   530 patients have waited there last year for liver transplants alone.

        2.   Eighteen percent, or 95 people, died waiting.

    D.   Public misconceptions contribute to the lack of donors.

        1.   "People who are rich and famous are bumped to the top of transplant lists."

        2.   "Doctors won't try as hard to save potential donors."

        3.   "There are already enough donors available."

This gives us a fairly complete organization of thought. You don't have every word you're going to say—in other words, it's not simply a manuscript broken up with Roman numerals and letters to *look* like an outline. For instance, for each public misconception you'll have statistics and stories to counter it.

Your outline doesn't contain everything you'll say; it just has enough material that someone reading it who didn't hear the speech can follow the line of thought. That rule of thumb guides us not only in using complete sentences (a phrase outline only makes sense to the writer—and even then, it often represents only vaguely thought-out ideas, which leads to lack of confidence and stumbling around in front of the audience), but in determining the depth of the outline.

The next step, which we won't flesh out here, is to do the same thing with Main Point II (and III, and IV, etc.). *Then* you write your introduction and your conclusion. Add your Works Cited (for instance, the complete reference for the *Health Index* articles you drew from), and you have a complete, full-sentence outline that serves you well in preparing for your speech.

The Outline Is *Not* the Speech

Sometimes a student won't be ready or able to deliver her speech, but she'll offer to give the teacher her outline. She may be trying to prove she was ready, which could be a legitimate concern. Other times, though, such a speaker may want the teacher to accept the outline *in place* of him doing his speech. He'll even say, "Here's my speech."

Let's be clear. The outline is only the basis, or the preparation, for the speech. It is not the speech. The speech is far more than just the outline.

Think of the difference between your favorite song as performed by your favorite band and what that song looks like reduced to paper. Some of you read music;

others may be familiar with "guitar tabs." Surely no one thinks that what's on the paper is the song! It represents the song, and helps the musician perform the song, but it's not the song.

Think of your preparation outline as the composer's sheet music, and your speaking outline as the guitar tab, and you'll have a pretty good idea of the relationship among the preparation outline, the speaking outline, and the speech itself.

Study questions
1. What is the purpose of the Body of the speech?
2. Why should your preparation outline be done in full sentences?
3. What function does the thesis fulfill for organizing your speech?
4. Should you or should you not take your outline to the lectern? Why?

Guidelines for an
Extemporaneous Speech Outline

TITLE OF SPEECH: All speeches must be titled. **Place your title here..**

GENERAL PURPOSE (METHOD OF PRESENTATION): to inform, to entertain, to demonstrate, to persuade by making in-roads, to convince, to actuate. **List one of these purposes here.**

SPECIFIC PURPOSE (AUDIENCE OUTCOME): What particular response do you want to evoke from your audience? **Write this sentence and fill in the blank here:** At the end of my speech I want my audience to_____.

INTRODUCTION

I. **INTEREST STEP** (ALSO CALLED "ICE BREAKER" OR "ATTEN-TION GETTER"): Use the beginning of your speech to capture the audience's interest and to stress the importance of the topic. You must tell on your outline how you are going to accomplish this step. List the technique(s) that you use in the appropriate place marked "technique." **Write a one sentence summary of your interest step here.**

TECHNIQUE: Use one of the techniques listed in the book here.

II. **THESIS SENTENCE:** The thesis sentence is one simple declarative statement which summarizes your speech. This statement is the crux of your speech. **Write your thesis sentence here.**

III. **CLARIFICATION:** This step can include definitions, background material, or any other information necessary for your audience to have a clear understanding of your thesis. **Write a one sentence summary of your clarification here.**

IV.   **PREVIEW STEP:** This step relates the main points of the speech to the audience members to facilitate understanding of proof of the thesis. "Tell them what you are going to tell them." **Write a one sentence transition statement here.**

BODY

I.   **MAIN POINT:** Each main point discussed in the body of the speech is a major division of the thesis. Each main point proves a part of the thesis by the method listed below. State your main point and then give *evidence* to support it: **Write your main point of proof in simple sentence form here.**

      A.   **EVIDENCE:** STATISTICS, EXAMPLES, QUOTATIONS FROM AUTHORITY, ANALOGIES, AND AUDIO/VISUAL AIDS are all forms of evidence. Use one of them at this point in proving a main point. **Write one simple sentence stating your evidence here.**

      B.   **REASONING** (EVIDENCE + REASONING = PROOF): After stating your main point and giving your evidence, explain how your evidence relates to your thesis. **Summarize the explanation of your evidence here in one simple sentence.**

      C.   **RELATIONSHIP TO THESIS:** Make sure you show how your proven main point relates to your thesis. Don't leave the relationship of main point to thesis for your audience to figure out. **Directly connect your proof (evidence plus reasoning) to your thesis in one simple transition sentence here.**

NOTE: Further main points and their proof should usually be put in the same format as Main Point I is shown here. Below is demonstrated a possible variation if you have more than one piece of evidence for a main point

II.   **MAIN POINT:** You follow the formula listed under MAIN POINT I for each main point in the body of your speech. If you have more than one piece of evidence for a main point, follow the formula for each piece of evidence: **Always write in simple sentence format.**

    A.   State sub-point of main point here
        1.   give evidence for sub-point
        2.   give reasoning for sub-point
        3.   show relationship of sub-point to main point and to the thesis.
    B.   State second sub-point of main point here.
        1.   give evidence
        2.   give reasoning
        3.   show relationship

III.   **MAIN POINT:** You should have three main points (see box at end of chapter), and at least three forms of evidence, for the body of each speech. You may have as many as five main points. Each main point and its proof should follow the format shown above.

CONCLUSION

I.   **SUMMARY STEP:** This step is similar to the preview step in the introduction. It reiterates the main points of argument. "Tell them what you have told them." **Write a one sentence summary here.**

II.   **RESTATEMENT OF THESIS:** Repeat the thesis often during the speech. It is the statement that you want your audience to remember and accept. **Write a re-statement of your thesis here.**

III.   **APPEAL:** This step is much like the interest step in the introduction. The final appeal is the lasting impression that you leave on your audience. It uses the same type of technique as the interest step. You must list the technique that you use. **Summarize your final appeal here in one sentence.**

TECHNIQUE: List the one used here.

NOTE: Until you have mastered the structure of an extemporaneous speech outline, you should follow these guidelines *exactly*. **EACH SEGMENT OF THE OUTLINE MUST BE WRITTEN IN COMPLETE, DECLARA-TIVE SENTENCES.**

What's the Minimum?

There is some disagreement among the authors and among other writers about how many main points should be the minimum. Therefore, in one place in the chapter we set two as the minimum, and elsewhere recommend three.

Rather than settle on one or the other or compromise (two and a half?), we decided to explain the thinking behind the numbers. One thing we're absolutely agree on is that you can't have just one main point! If you do, you don't have a main point, you have a thesis. *Any* idea can be broken down into components.

We strongly recommend three as a minimum. In rare situations, two may work best—but usually it just marks you as lazy. However, it won't get you jailed by the speech police. One main point will get you in trouble—if not legally, then at least with your audience.

So think about it, understand your subject more deeply, and come up with at least three main points. It'll do you and your audience good.

<table>
<tr><td>Chapter
10</td><td></td></tr>
</table>

Supporting Materials

W hen we say "supporting material" you probably almost immediately say, "Oh, sure, I know what that is. That's like statistics and quotations and stuff."

While that's true in a way, it's only true at a superficial level. We need to go deeper than that.

If organization is like the skeleton of a speech, then supporting material is like the muscles and blood. Supporting material makes the speech live and move.

> ## Supporting material is what actually *makes* your points.

Supporting material is what actually *makes* your points. You don't *make* your point by *stating* your point, you make it by supporting it. Supporting material establishes or proves or illustrates or expands upon your point. Supporting material makes your audience understand the point, or care about the point, or believe the point.

Supporting material makes up the bulk of your speech, although without the skeleton of the organization it wouldn't do much. Muscle attached to a strong skeleton yields a living, moving creature. Muscle unattached just yields a pile of meat. Interesting, perhaps, but not moving.

You have some existing knowledge of supporting material, since you've survived the American educational system to this point. Rather than go over a lot of familiar items like statistics and quotations, we'll concentrate on learning a system that enables you to *use* those familiar techniques effectively.

Two Major Types

We'll classify the mostly familiar ways of supporting points into two major categories in order to figure out when to use those ways most effectively. The two major categories of supporting material are:
- Hard supporting material
- Soft supporting material

No judgment is involved here. We don't mean that one is strong and the other weak, or one is difficult and the other easy. The categories have to do with psychological feel.

First, let's explain what each category involves. Then we'll see what difference the understanding makes.

Hard Supporting Material

Hard support tends to be objective in nature. "Objective" is not a magic, holy word, although some in our society seem to think it is, as if only that which is objective has any value. "Objective" just means that different observers observing the same phenomenon tend to report it in about the same way.

Definitions of traffic death. Some accidental deaths obviously fall under this heading: if someone dies in a head-on collision on the Interstate, it's definitely a traffic death. Some obviously are *not*: someone electrocuted in a hot tub in a remote Smoky Mountains cabin is *not* a traffic death. What about a pedestrian walking on the side of the road? How about a farmer plowing in a field with a tractor who is killed when a passing truck flings up a rock from the road surface that hits him in the head? (That actually happened a few years ago.) What if the person in the hot tub died because a car hit a transformer that caused a surge in the electric grid that blew out a breaker in his hot tub five miles away? The point here is not how Tennessee defines traffic death, but rather the need to agree on a definition.

For instance, if we want to look at traffic deaths in the state of Tennessee, we can do a little research and find that there were 1,217 traffic deaths in the state in 1998 (*Tennessee Anytime*). As long as we agree on the definition of

94

Effect	Hard Support	Soft Support
Nature of material	Objective	Subjective
Effect on audience	Convinces	Moves
Effect on point	Proves	Clarifies or "realizes"

Figure 10.1: Hard and soft supporting material and its usage.

traffic deaths, we can count the bodies and come up with the same figure, whether we're Democrat or Republican, religious or not, educated or not (assuming we can count). We might disagree about the cause, or about the implications, but we'll agree on the number.

Because audience members view such information as objective, it has the effect in their minds of proving the point you're trying to make, and therefore tends to convince them.

It's important to remember that "convincing" is primarily an intellectual activity. So what? Think about your own experience. Aren't you convinced that you would be healthier if you exercised more? Or stopped smoking? Or cut down on fat in your diet? Or ... you get the point. Do you actually follow through on those beliefs? All the time?

(Disclaimer: there certainly *are* people who follow through on these beliefs. However, we all recognize the number of people who act on these beliefs is far smaller than the number of people who say they hold these beliefs.)

Keep that in mind as we look at the other major category.

Soft Supporting Material

Soft support tends to be subjective in nature. That's almost a dirty word in our society. You can win arguments by saying, "That's just your subjective opinion." But in the context of human communication (and especially in persuasion, as we'll see shortly), "subjective" not only is OK at times, it is even ***essential***! "Subjective" means that the information *must* be interpreted in light of personal experience for it to have any meaning to the listener. That is the very thing that gives soft support its power.

You see, if you're trying to *prove* something with soft support, it won't work. This is what gives it a bad name in academic circles: most of the time in writing a paper or doing an academic presentation, you're trying to prove something, and as we're already seeing, if you want to prove something, you'd better use hard supporting material. But when we're communicating with other people, we need to go past just proving something—if we're going to get people out of mere intellectual agreement and into action, that is.

Because soft support gets interpreted in light of personal experience, it makes the information, well, *personal*. It takes it out of the abstract and makes it clear to the listener, makes it *real*—hence, we say it "realizes" the point. Because it has become clear and real, it tends to move the listener. It's no longer merely intellectual. It's no coincidence that "motion" and "emotion" are such similar words. "Emotion" literally is "that which moves us."

Examples of Categories

Let's take those familiar types of supporting material and see where they fit into this scheme. We'll then be able to see more clearly how the scheme helps us choose supporting material based on what we want to accomplish at a given point in the speech.

When we talked about *hard supporting material*, we used **statistics** to explain what it is. Most audiences view statistics as objective, so for them it proves the information and convinces them. (Note that we're always saying things like "audience members *view* statistics as being objective" rather than "statistics are objective." We're not interested in the old argument about whether there really is such a thing as objectivity; it doesn't matter, because whether there is or isn't we are only interested in how the audience views it, which determines the effects on them.) If you want to prove to the audience that seat belts save lives, trot out statistics that prove that far fewer people die in accidents involving people wearing seat belts.

For similar reasons, audiences view **scientific reports** as being objective. They know enough about scientific method to hold this opinion.

For example, let's imagine for just a moment that you are a nuclear physicist at Oak Ridge National Laboratories (it's a great stretch of the imagination, but try). Let's say that you believe you have observed cold fusion happening in a mayonnaise jar in my refrigerator (there's definitely *something* going on in there). You set up an experiment under controlled conditions, observe the outcome, and publish my findings.

Another physicist in, say, Oregon reads my report, sets up a similar experiment, gets the same results, and publishes her findings also. Yet another physicist in Bombay, India, reads both our reports, sets up a similar experiment, gets the same results, and publishes his findings also.

It doesn't matter that we all might have different religious beliefs, different political ideas, different social backgrounds, different ages, etc. If we've set the experiment up correctly, we ought to get nearly the same results (at least, that's the assumption). Because audience members know this about scientific reports, they tend to treat them as being objective.

> **I'm more likely to *move* them to action by giving them a specific example or telling them a story.**

The next example more clearly shows that it's the audience's viewpoint that counts rather than whether the material is "really" objective. Audiences tend to treat **expert testimony** as being objective. This type of material would be like you (the physicist again) standing in front of an audience and saying, "I've been a physicist for 25 years. I hold the Nobel Peace Prize for Mayonnaise Fusion. And, in my opinion, Hellman's mayonnaise produces the best nuclear reaction." You're not turning to other physicists, you're simply standing on long years of experience. This is a little chancy and depends on the audience buying your credentials. But if they do buy them, they don't view what you've said as "just an opinion." They view it as an *informed* opinion and treat it as if it is relatively free of bias.

On the other hand, the most common example of *soft supporting material* is the **example**. Examples are single instances of a more general pattern. (Note: when you say "My friends all say I'm outgoing," you're not giving an example; you're simply stating a general pattern in a different way than just saying "I'm outgoing.") Similar to examples, but more developed in structure, is the **narrative** or story. If I want to get my audience members to

98

actually *wear* seat belts rather than simply agree that doing so is a good idea, I'm more likely to *move* them to action by giving them a specific example or telling them a story.

For instance, one of the authors could tell the audience about a friend of his named Johnny (that really was his name) who was a senior when the author was a junior. One day a couple of weeks before graduation he and three of his friends hopped in his Mustang and headed out to the old Laneview school to play basketball. They topped a hill and ran head-on into a 3/4-ton truck full of beans. You don't move one of those with a Mustang. Johnny, who was not wearing his seat belt, was ejected through the windshield into the engine of the truck and was killed instantly. The guy in the back seat behind him, also without a seat belt, was thrown out of the car. A lot of people think they're safer without a seat belt because they'll be thrown out of harm's way, but hitting the ground at 70 miles per hour hurts. He died a few days later from massive internal injuries, just days before graduation.

The person in the front seat on the right had his seat belt on, and received a broken arm and a broken leg. The person in the back seat behind him had a few cuts and bruises.

Obviously we could get a lot more out of this story, but even from this relatively unemotional telling you can probably feel a greater effect than from a bunch of statistics. That's because, even though you didn't know Johnny (it was nearly 30 years ago and 400 miles away), you know someone like him, or you know *about* a similar situation. You interpret that story in light of your experience, and so it has a more gut-level effect.

Of course, the story doesn't prove anything. You have to go to hard support for that. But the story is more likely to move people to action *after* they've been convinced by your hard support.

Likewise, the **analogy** helps to clarify information and make it real, even though it doesn't prove anything. The very word suggests its function: it is not logic, it is *ana*logic—other than logic.

For instance, if you're trying to explain to a group of fifth-graders how electricity works, you could say that electricity moves through a wire in a way similar to the way water moves through a hose. It has direction to it—that's called current. It has pressure behind it—that's called voltage. A thin hose allows less water through than does a thick hose. The same thing is true of wires.

This comparison will help them understand electricity, but it won't prove anything about electricity. You couldn't conclude, for example, that electrons must be wet. One of the first fallacies logicians learn is the fallacy of arguing by analogy.

So don't try to prove anything with an analogy. But don't hesitate to clarify something that way.

It would be nice and clean if we could get all kinds of testimony to fit under one heading or the other. But we can't. Expert testimony, which we've already discussed, fits under hard supporting material because the audience views it as objective. But we have at least two other kinds of testimony that fit under soft supporting material because the audience tends to be moved by it.

On the surface **prestige testimony** sounds similar to expert testimony. It's true that some people fit both categories. When Michael Jordan does a commercial for basketball shoes, his testimony is both expert testimony and prestige testimony. He certainly is an expert in basketball (for which the shoes are a tool), and he's also quite recognizable and well known. Advertisers like to use such celebrities as spokespeople because they can get two effects from one support.

But when Michael Jordan does a commercial for a long-distance telephone company, he is not speaking as an expert. He's not a telecommunications engineer. His contribution to that particular commercial comes through just having a recognizable face. People watching think, "I wanna be like Mike," and are moved (at least to some degree) to switch long-distance providers.

> **Lay testimony and the "band wagon."** Of course, people don't *consciously* think, "I'll bet I would too!" If they did, they might then think, "Why? What makes me think that?" Nevertheless, the band wagon effect is a powerful one. When your mother asked you, "If all your friends jumped off a bridge, does that mean you would too?" she knew the real answer was, "Probably so." High school guidance counselors get very nervous after there has been a suicide in their school, because (along with the grief) there is a much higher probability of someone *else* committing suicide after the first one.

Is there anything logical about that? Just because Michael Jordan likes MCI, does it mean the service is good? It may be, but getting Michael to say so doesn't prove it. From the advertiser's standpoint, that doesn't matter, because they're not trying to prove it, they're just trying to get you to move.

Another well-known advertiser illustrates the use of **lay testimony** in their commercials. When McDonald's shows scenes of older people enjoying breakfast at McDonald's, they're appealing to people of that same age group. Although no one in the commercial is famous, the target market members look at the commercial and say,

"They're like me, and they seem to be having a good time. I'll bet I would too!"

Put It Together

You have to have both kinds of support. Our educational system has emphasized hard supporting material, because most of the time they were concerned with teaching us how to *prove* things. Don't start ignoring hard supporting material; just gather the soft supporting material too.

> **Pick the kind of support you need based on what you need to accomplish at that point.**

If you just have hard supporting material in a speech you may convince people without moving them to do anything about it. If you sell a brand of automobile that you really believe in, one you think really does solve people's need for transportation in an economical and safe manner, then you fail to serve the public when you fail to sell. If someone leaves your showroom intellectually convinced your brand is best, but they leave without the car, you haven't done them any good (and you haven't earned a commission, either).

On the other hand, if you just have soft supporting material you may get people all stirred up and emotional at the time. They may even verbally commit to do something. But after they've cooled down, in the absence of hard support they can't think of a reason to follow through. So they don't.

So when you are writing your speech, don't just gather the familiar statistics. Write down the stories and analogies too. Then, think about what you're trying to accomplish *at that particular point* in your speech. For main point number I, for example, your major task may be convincing the audience that there really is a problem. "Convincing." That means you need hard supporting material. Later, in main point number II under subpoint B, you may be mainly trying to clarify a difficult concept. "Clarify." That calls for soft supporting material.

There was a famous advertising experiment carried out back in the 1960s that illustrates the usefulness of this chart. The experiment involved showing two very similar commercials to two sets of demographically identical viewers. The first one showed a man in a white coat with a stethoscope around his neck. He said, "Hi, I'm Doctor Whatsis,

Failure to follow through. Some (though not all) of the "electronic ministries" have problems with this. They are very good at showing striking, emotional photographs of starving children to stir our guilt feelings and get us to promise to send money. But at the end of the month, when you've cooled down and it's time to write the check, you won't follow through if you can't think of a good reason. Some "electronic ministries" have less than a 10 percent follow-through rate, i.e., fewer than 10 percent of the people who say they'll send money actually send it.

Contrast this with an effective fund-raising group like the Save the Children foundation. One of the authors remembers sponsoring a child through them. He says, "At the time Sally Struthers was their spokesperson. She started out talking about six million starving people in Ethiopia. This is hard support, something I could understand intellectually. But I can't get a handle on six million of *anything* on a gut level. I just couldn't fathom it. Even if I sent them everything I owned, it wouldn't have been a drop of water in the ocean.

"So Sally mostly talked about a specific child. I could imagine making a difference to one child.

"Furthermore, they didn't talk in terms of $180 a year to support this child. Those of you with children know that $180 a year is phenomenally cheap. I wish I could get by on that every two weeks for

Continued next page

103

Continued from previous page

our kid! Still, I couldn't just reach in my wallet for it, and it was an abstract figure anyhow. They could have just broken it down to $15 a month (and they did say that at some point), but they went past that. They said we could support this child "for the cost of a can of soda a day." That's really concrete, something I can *see* in my mind's eye. I could imagine giving up a can of soda a day in order to feed this child for a year.

"When we contributed, we also got real photographs (I'm a skeptic; I checked to make sure they were individual photographs instead of mass-produced copies from an offset press) that showed the child growing and getting healthier. We received hand-written letters that came from an interpreter who wrote on behalf of the mother. (Some of the rip-off charities send letters too, but they often purport to come from the child. Give me a break—a six-year-old in Ethiopia who knows how to write English?)

"Along with the letters came business reports showing, for instance, that they only spent about 5 percent of their income on management expenses (vs. up to 90 percent for some bogus "charities"). That provided hard support to convince me they were on the level.

"The powerful combination led to us sponsoring this child for two years, until our business went bust and we needed someone to buy rice for us."

and I'm the chief of surgery at Mt. Sinai Hospital. When my patients experience mild discomfort, I prescribe for them Bayer aspirin [holds up the product]." The other one also showed a man in a white coat with a stethoscope around his neck. He said, "Hi, I'm not a real doctor, but I play one on TV." (Fame is fleeting. I can't remember the actor's name to save my life, but at the time he was very recognizable because of his role in a television show—a soap opera, if I remember correctly.) Understand that he's not trying to fool us; he tells us right up front that he's not a real doctor. Then he said, "When I have a headache, I use Bayer aspirin."

Guess which one sold more aspirin? If you chose the actor, you're right. That commercial sold almost twice as much aspirin as the other one.

It's not because we're gullible. After all, the guy told us he was an actor. Think about it in terms of our categories. What kind of material did the real doctor provide? Expert testimony, right? That's a kind of hard supporting material. What does hard supporting material do for us? That's right, it convinces us. Do you have to be convinced that aspirin will help a headache? You probably believe that already. The task for the advertiser is not to convince us that the product works. (Note: that may very well *be* the case for less familiar products.)

The task for the advertiser is this: when we're standing in front of that shelf at Wal-Mart and there are 47 brands of aspirin, all of which are pretty much alike, to get us to reach out and pick up his particular brand. It's not a logical decision in the first place; it's a *psycho*logical one. In other words, the advertiser needs to *move* us to a specific action.

Our categories tell us that soft support moves the audience, so we could have predicted that the prestige testimony (the recognizable actor) would have worked better than the expert testimony (the real doctor).

Study questions

1. What are the two major categories of supporting material? What are each used for in the speech?
2. How are different types of testimony perceived by the audience?
3. How do you decide on the type of support needed?

Works Cited in This Chapter

"Traffic Deaths Down for Third Straight Year."
TennesseeAnytime: The Official Site Of The State Of Tennessee. May 24, 1999. http://www.state.tn.us/safety/ news%20releases/memorialday99.html (25 June 2001).

Chapter 11

Language: Verbal Aspects of Public Speaking

When we were small, we heard the saying, "Sticks and stones may break my bones, but words will never hurt me." We knew it was a lie even then. Words have a unique kind of power, which cultures around the world have recognized. Although it's an oversimplification, it's not far off the mark to argue that World War II was a war between effective communicators.

Adolph Hitler harnessed the power of effective speaking to move an entire nation of people into the tragedy of the war, while across the English Channel another effective communicator named Winston Churchill talked with his people about blood and toil and sweat and tears, and moved them to resist the Nazi efforts. (This example also shows that the tools of communication may be used for good or ill, and so should be accompanied by a study of ethics!)

> **"The ability to make a good speech is a great gift to the people from the Maker, Owner of all things..."**

As a quote in a catalog for a Native American community college shows, the Oglala Sioux believed the power of speech had divine origins, saying "the ability to make a good speech is a great gift to the people from the Maker, Owner of all things" (Oglala Sioux Community College, p. 2).

In Chapter 1 we pointed out that words have no meaning in and of themselves, but are simply symbols that stand for ideas. This doesn't mean words have no power, however. In fact, it is their very symbolic nature that gives them their power, because it is much easier to manipulate symbols than actual ideas or objects. Words have such power simply because we give them such.

Words Can Make You See Things

Anyone who has ever sat around a campfire listening to a gifted storyteller weave ghost tales knows about this one. Written words can paint mental pictures, but spoken words have even more power in this regard.

I remember as a child hearing my dad talk about his experiences in World War II. The walls of the living room faded away for me and were replaced by a sandy Italian beach at dawn as bombs dropped in the water beside the landing boat where Dad huddled with his comrades. I felt the water splash and heard the thump as the boat right next to us exploded from a direct hit and saw the body parts land in our midst. I even felt a measure of his pain as he finally talked about these things 40 years after they happened.

The power to make audiences see things that are not right in front of them is a power indeed.

Words Can Make You Feel Things

Is there a song that comes on the radio that makes you cry? Certainly the music contributes to this—the rhythm, the speed, the harmony. On the other hand, instrumentals without vocals move few people to tears. The words of the song are empowered by the music, but it is the words that stir the emotions.

When I was seven years old I would listen to "Puff the Magic Dragon" on the radio and cry. My parents were mystified. To this day that old song about change and growing up gets the same reaction, although I generally don't express it so unambiguously.

Words Can Make You Do Things

You have been on both the giving and receiving end of this. If you've ever talked your little brother into doing something that got him in trouble, if you've ever been convinced to buy something from a door-to-door salesperson, if you've ever sent money to a noble cause you heard about on television, if you've ever gone out on a date—you know that words can get you to do things.

Words Can Confuse You

When they don't seem to connect with reality, words can confuse you. The structure may suggest it's a legitimate sentence, but it still doesn't make sense. Consider the following headlines from actual newspapers (note that current newspaper headline style generally uses capitalization like a sentence instead of like a book title):

- **Boring woman of the year** (story about a woman named Alberta Boring (an employee of our college, in fact) who was named Woman of the Year in her hometown)
- **British study finds less traffic when road closes** (reporting on a study that found that closing the road didn't stop traffic, only lessened it)
- **Sun or rain expected today, dark tonight** (no kidding?)

More real headlines
"Fund Set Up For Beating Victim's Kin"
"United Hires Ex-Chairman Of United"
"Animal Rights Group To Hold Meeting At Steakhouse"
"Honeymoon Trip On Titanic Was Eventful Night"
"Do It Yourself Pregnancy Kit To Go On Sale"
"Blind Woman Gets New Kidney From Dad She Hasn't Seen in Years"
"New Bar Exam to Include Test of Legal Skills"
"Study Finds Sex/Pregnancy Link"
"Heat Wave Linked To Temperatures"
"Hospitals Are Sued By 7 Foot Doctors"
"Lack Of Brains Hinders Research"
"Killer Sentenced To Die For Second Time In Ten Years"
"Chef Throws His Heart Into Helping Feed Needy"
"Cincinnati Dry Cleaner Sentenced In Suit"
"Local High School Drop Outs Cut In Half"
"High Speed Train Could Reach Valley In Five Years"
"Two Convicts Evade Noose; Jury Hung"
"Police Nab Student With Pair Of Pliers"
"Marijuana Issue Sent To Joint Committee"

- **New electric car would run on gasoline** (story about what is actually a hybrid car that uses gasoline to run a generator)
- **Jane Fonda to teens: Use head to avoid pregnancy** (um, actually, she said you could avoid getting pregnant if you just acted sensibly)
- **Actor sent to jail for not finishing sentence** (from our local paper)
- **Fresno council to talk about talking less at meetings**

Although it's not a headline, this classified ad illustrates a sentence that may confuse more than communicate (it ran with an address from California, in case that explains anything): "WANTED: Somebody to go back in time with me. This is not a joke. P.O. Box XXX, Oakview, CA 93022. You'll get paid after we get back. Must bring own weapons. Safety not guaranteed. I have only done this once before."

Using Words Effectively

Although you should definitely *not* memorize your speech, paying attention to your habitual use of language and developing more effective habits will not only help you give better speeches, but also to communicate more effectively in conversations, at home, and at work. These specific suggestions should help the process.

Tape Yourself

Writer/speaker/sales trainer Zig Ziglar has said that a professional salesperson who doesn't own a tape recorder with which to tape her own presentation costs herself at least $20,000 a year in revenue. He makes this claim based on the idea that a professional salesperson's most effective tool is his voice. This bit of advice will obviously help you improve your paralanguage skills (see Chapters 12 and

13), but it will also help you to learn about your use of language.

Obviously, it will help you to grow if you tape your speeches and listen to them later. You can also learn something about your use of language (as well as delivery) if you tape yourself in conversation (be sure your friends know what you're doing, and why!). You can also tape yourself during telephone conversations (again, make the other party aware that you're taping) with a small device that attaches to your telephone and a tape recorder.

To improve your language abilities, listen specifically to the way you use words, and compare what you hear with the other suggestions here.

> "The difference between the almost right word and the right word is the difference between the lightning bug and the lightning."

Be Accurate

Even though meaning is in people, not in words (see Chapter 1), you communicate most clearly when you use words in the way that most other people use them. A dictionary is a useful tool in finding out how other people tend to use a particular word. Make sure you use the "correct" term when you talk to an audience. Using one the audience will perceive as "incorrect" can lead you to quickly lose credibility.

For instance, in East Tennessee we frequently hear speakers say "ideal" when they mean "idea." If a speaker says, "I had no ideal it would work that way," it leaves the impression that he really doesn't know what he's talking about. As Mark Twain once said, "The difference between the almost right word and the right word is the difference between the lightning bug and the lightning." (Note: You usually see this quoted slightly differently. We looked it up in *The Columbia World of Quotations.* It's one of those things that everybody knows, but isn't quite right. Look things up.)

By the way, "went" is not a synonym for "said." Neither is "goes" or "like." Do not recount anything resembling the following:

> *So I'm like, "I can't believe this is happening to me!" And he goes, "Well, duh!" And I was just so, "You're such a doofus!" And he went, "So what are you, Einstein?"*
> No. Not exactly.

Use Vivid Words

While remaining accurate (that is, don't exaggerate), use colorful words. Don't say, "He hit the ball and went around the bases." Say, "He slammed the ball to right field and tore around the bases."

Be Concrete and Specific

This will also help you to be vivid. Don't be satisfied to describe your pet as "a dog" when "a cocker spaniel" will be appropriate. Don't throw soft descriptors such as "thousands of people homeschool their kids every day" at us. Dig a little and report, "According to the Homeschool Legal Defense Association, there are around one million homeschooled students in the United States."

Use Active Voice

Check to see how often you use some form of the verb "to be." It's not wrong to do so—I just used a form of "to be" to start this sentence when I said, "it's not wrong." Sometimes it's the best form. But you can add punch to

your sentences and to your speech by avoiding it as much as possible. For instance, compare the next two sentences:
1. There are several ways to cook eggs.
2. You can cook eggs several ways.

The second way has just a bit more punch to it.

Active voice has an actor. Passive voice usually doesn't. Academic writing often uses passive voice, because the writers think it makes them sound more objective. Government reports also use it a lot, for the same reason—and maybe because it lets the writer avoid naming who is responsible. "The troop ship was lost." Who lost it? If I use passive voice, I don't have to say.

Nevertheless, "he hit the ball" sounds more interesting than "the ball was hit," even if you say "the ball was hit by him."

Eliminate Clutter

Have you ever noticed how coat hangers tend to multiply in your closet? Words can act the same way—they proliferate like tree fungus unless you keep them trimmed. When words multiply, they lose their punch.

This is probably bad news for folks who have developed the habit of padding their writing as a means of surviving the academic system. You've spent a lifetime treating the teacher's "write a 500-word essay" guideline as a primary goal. This is not new. In the 1950s Paul McHenry Roberts wrote an often-reprinted essay entitled "How to Say Nothing in 500 Words." Even then students engaged in the same padding practices. He said:

> How, he asks himself, is he to achieve this staggering total? Obviously by never using one word when he can somehow work in ten.
>
> He is therefore seldom content with a

plain statement like "Fast driving is dangerous." This has only four words in it. He takes thought, and the sentence becomes:

> *In my opinion, fast driving is dangerous.*

Better, but he can do better still:

> *In my opinion, fast driving would seem to be rather dangerous.*

If he is really adept, it may come out:

> *In my humble opinion, though I do not claim to be an expert on this complicated subject, fast driving, in most circumstances, would seem to be rather dangerous in many respects, or at least so it would seem to me.*

Thus four words have been turned into forty, and not an iota of content has been added.

Now this is a way to go about reaching five hundred words, and if you are content with a "D" grade, it is as good a way as any. But if you aim higher, you must work differently. Instead of stuffing your sentences with straw, you must try steadily to get rid of the padding, to make your sentences lean and tough.

Clutter comes from more than just academic pressures, though. Government tends this way also. At least since the Nixon administration we have had to put up with people saying "at this point in time" instead of "now."

George Bush (the elder) gave us "at this juncture" rather than "now." Others have contributed "at the present time," "currently," and "presently."

Why not just say "now"? Or just use the present tense? You don't need to say, "We are experiencing heavy quantities of precipitation at this point in time." It works fine to say, "It's raining heavily!"

Clutter and euphemism go together. The military has given us "collateral damage" when they used to say "casualties"—itself a word they coined when they didn't want to say "dead people." Thus "collateral damage" has become the preferred term for "people we didn't mean to kill." Notice that clutter isn't necessarily longer. "Collateral damage" has fewer words but less content.

"Omit need-less words."

Nevertheless, in general prefer the shorter, simpler words and phraseology. Compare the following pairs of words and note which have more punch.

- implement | do
- initial | first
- initiate | start
- categorize | sort
- facilitate | ease
- referred to as | called
- in order to | to
- due to the fact that | because
- for the purpose of | for
- smile happily | smile
- tall skyscraper | skyscraper
- dialogue with | talk to
- interface with | talk to

Beginning a sentence leads a lot of people to clutter. "There is" often adds unnecessary weight. "There is a way to get rid of clutter easily." Just say, "You can get rid of

115

clutter easily." Look hard at the adverb—you likely don't need it. "It is interesting to note that…"—just note it.

The classic text on this is *The Elements of Style* (Strunk and White). Although it deals with writing, the principle applies to spoken language. Entry 17 famously says, "Omit needless words."

Use the "Carson Principle"

Although Johnny Carson has not chaired *The Tonight Show* for a long time, many people still remember the way he conducted the show. A standard feature had him making a soft, open-ended statement such as, "It was really windy today." The audience, on cue, said as a group, "How windy was it?"

For that particular joke, Carson said, "It was so windy, I saw a robin lay the same egg three times."

You might have to think about it a minute, but when you do, you'll get a very clear (though not pretty) picture. (If you don't get the picture, see the box at the end.)

The idea behind the "Carson Principle" deals not with humor, but with clarity. Your audience will likely *not ask* about something you tell them that is simply fuzzy. Anticipate their questions. If you're tempted to use such softphraseology as "every year hundreds of students graduate from Pellissippi State," back up, do the research, and instead report "650 students graduated from Pellissippi State in the spring of 2002, according to the school's Community Relations Office."

The Carson Principle not only communicates more clearly, but helps you to *use* time rather than simply fill it or "pad" it. When you use the Carson Principle, you won't have to struggle to come up with 500 words, so to speak. Your problem becomes not how to meet the minimum time requirements of your speech assignment, but rather how to get it within the maximum time. While you're doing that, the information will hold your audience's interest, and will make the experience a pleasant one for you, as well as for your audience.

Summary

When you watch a master carpenter use a hammer, it obviously differs from an amateur's use. Amateurs pound and pound, bend many nails, start over again, and waste a lot of time and materials. Master carpenters hit the nail simply and forcefully, driving the point home with two or three strokes.

We won't stretch the metaphor too far. Just keep the image in mind, and don't waste words. They are your primary tools. Make them count.

Study questions
1. Why do words have power?
2. Explain why accuracy matters.
3. Explain three ways you personally could eliminate clutter in your language.
4. What is the Carson Principle, and why is it useful for speakers?

About that bird: Imagine the bird facing *into* a very strong wind. Now imagine the bird turning the other way, laying an egg, then experiencing the trauma of having the wind, well, put it back where it came from. Now imagine the rather determine bird doing this twice more. That would be quite windy, wouldn't it? Now try not to think about it too much.

Works Cited in Chapter

Roberts, Paul McHenry. "How to Say Nothing in 500 Words." *Apostate Café.* 2 June 2002 <http://www.apostate.com/writing/nothing.html>.

Strunk, William, Jr., and E. B. White. *The Elements of Style.* 4th ed. Boston: Allyn & Bacon, 2000.

"The Lakota Family." *Bulletin of Oglala Sioux Community College, 1980-81.* Pine Ridge, S.D.

Chapter 12

Delivery: Nonverbal Aspects of Public Speaking

"You don't have to say it to convey it." Nonverbal communication (NVC) is an important aspect of communicating with our fellow human beings. In fact, over half of all communication is nonverbal. Nonverbal communication is the conscious or subconscious transmission and reception of unspoken messages (Birdwhistle). In many cases *what* we say may not be as important as *how* we say it. Understanding nonverbal communication helps us better understand and communicate with the people around us.

The study of nonverbal communication is a vast and growing field providing fascinating insights into human behavior which many times reveals true emotions or feelings. Sometimes nonverbal communication is more revealing than spoken words. For example, we all have heard sayings and phrases that clearly demonstrate the importance of nonverbal communication, such as:

√ "Actions speak louder than words."

√ "It wasn't so much what he said, but how he said it."

√ "She had a look that could kill."

√ "Beauty is skin deep, but ugly goes to the bone."

There have been other phrases coined for nonverbal communication including "silent language," "body language," "facial language," "silent messages," and "beyond words."

Messages Without Words
in Public Speaking

A person can listen at 500-750 words per minute (wpm), but most people—particularly new speakers—speak at 150-250 wpm. This difference in rate leaves about 80 percent of the conscious brainpower of the listener free to concentrate elsewhere. Much of that concentration focuses on the voice and body actions of the speaker.

Getting the terms straight

When you see the components of communication broken down into three parts, "nonverbal" refers to those things that can be seen. When the components are broken down into two parts, "nonverbal" also includes the things that have to do with the use of the voice—the things called "paralanguage" in the three-part breakdown.

In a landmark study, Albert Mehrabian found that in a face-to-face interaction listeners received about 7 percent of the speaker's message directly from the words he spoke, 38 percent from his use of voice (called "vocalics" or "paralanguage"), and 55 percent from his body actions, gestures, and appearance (called "nonverbal").

Although popular literature has applied that study in ways Mehrabian never intended (Lapakko), numerous follow-up studies suggest that nonverbal communication makes up the bulk of our interaction. That makes sense when you realize the type of information nonverbal communication sends: "nonlogical" information such as how the speaker feels about his topic, his audience, and even himself. A seminal study by Alan Monroe long ago showed that audiences generally consider good delivery to equal good speaking. Arguably it is the reason you take a class in public speaking rather than an advanced composition class.

Nonverbal communication, then, is of prime importance to a speaker and to his audience.

There are several elements of nonverbal communication. For the purpose of practicality we shall discuss only those elements over which you may have some control and which you may find important in public speaking endeavors.

How Nonverbal Communication Influences Your Audience in Public Speaking

It is generally understood that in a professional context people are more receptive to a neatly dressed, well-groomed individual. A business-like appearance will add to your credibility as a speaker. Although you may not agree that people *should* be judged by the way they look, it is a fact of life that they are. You can use it to your advantage or ignore it at your peril! You are your own best visual aid.

Ethos, as defined by Aristotle, is the speaker's believability or credibility (see Chapter 15 for a more detailed discussion of ethos). A speaker must establish it each time she speaks. Furthermore, it's not really true that a speaker *has* credibility, but rather that the audience *perceives* the speaker as credible.

Politicians are a good example. Many people in our country are generally uninformed about political issues or the views of political candidates. However, generally speaking, most candidates have become experts at creating an illusion of "high ethos." They understand nonverbal communication and how to use it and have a command of human relations skills. Right or wrong, they have learned to play the ethos game and create an illusion of believability.

Nonverbal Communication Is Symbolic

Communication is the transmission or exchange of symbols that stand for ideas or information. Intentional communication is initiated when a person has a thought or message the speaker wants to transmit or convey to another person. The speaker translates thoughts into words, which are simply symbols for ideas, and uses these symbols as a means of transmitting the message to the receiver. The receiver in turn interprets or adds meaning to the words heard or read.

Even though nonverbal communication does not use words, it still uses symbols to stand for ideas and information. Pointing to indicate direction or using a thumbs-up gesture are obvious examples. Even such natural expressions as smiling are actually symbols rather than ideas. For true communication to take place, the symbols must represent the same ideas to the receiver as they do to the sender in order for the receiver to understand the intended message. If for any reason the receiver does not comprehend the message the sender intends to relate, the communication process is not complete.

Nonverbal Communication Defined

It seems useful to agree that **Nonverbal communication** should generally be defined as: *"messages expressed by other than linguistic means."* This definition would rule out sign languages and written symbols and words also. It also distinguishes certain aspects of the voice from those that aren't verbal. The parts that could be transcribed represent verbal aspects of the voice. The parts that you could detect if you heard an audiotape of a speaker talking in an unfamiliar language represent paralanguage and would fall into the broad category of nonverbal communication. Some of these assorted nonlinguistic noises could include sighs, laughs, speech volume, rate, pitch and so on.

Communication theorists agree that human beings send out messages even when we make an attempt not to communicate at all. In other words, the very attempt not to communicate communicates something. **The impossibility of not communicating is a very important point, because it means that each individual is a kind of transmitter that cannot be shut off**. Regardless of what we do, we ooze out information about ourselves.

Think about it for a minute, and examine yourself as you read this. If another individual observed you now, what messages would that person receive about you? Are you sitting or standing? Are you tense or relaxed? Are your eyes shut or wide open? What does your face communicate?

Try an experiment: make your face expressionless. Do people with expressionless faces send messages without words? If you play poker with someone who has been animatedly engaged in conversation, and she suddenly goes "expressionless," you know something, don't you? You know she either just got a really good hand or a really bad one. You will look for other cues to further focus the message, but she has definitely communicated something.

Observe a person sitting or even sleeping. Does that person communicate anything? Try the "You Can't Not

You Can't Not Communicate Experiment

Goal: To demonstrate that as human beings we all transmit messages about ourselves and about our environment continuously.

Things needed: Pen or pencil and something to write on; one partner for each participant.

Step 1: Find someone in class you don't know, find a place in the classroom, and face off for two minutes with your partner.

Step 2: Face your partner and do not say anything verbally. *Do not talk or laugh! This is crucial!*

Step 3: Next, honestly try your best for the next two minutes "not to reveal any messages back and forth."

Step 4: Last, be observant during this experiment and take notes about what perceptions and impressions you form about your partner. *Do not let your partner see what you have written down!* Discuss what happened with your partner.

Communicate Experiment" to really determine if it is possible to not communicate.

Unintentional Messages Without Words

As human beings we don't always intend to send nonverbal messages. Examine behaviors like stammering, sweating, frowning, or blushing. We are often unaware of these *"messages without words"* that we send out about ourselves. Others recognize these signs and make stereotypical interpretations about us based on these observations. Likewise, as a public speaker your audience will make observations and assumptions about your speaker ethos (believability), logos (presentation of facts), and pathos (emotional state of mind), based on the messages-without-words you transmit about yourself.

> *What you are speaks so loudly I cannot hear what you say.* —**Ralph Waldo Emerson**

Try the "Unintentional Messages Without Words Experiment" to determine what kind of *messages without words* you transmit unintentionally.

Your Voice Conveys Underlying Feelings

> *I understand a fury in your words, but not the words.* —**William Shakespeare, Othello**

The voice can indeed communicate messages without words. How we say or speak words can have as much importance as the actual symbolic meaning of these words. For example look at the various possible perception and interpretations from a single sentence just by changing the word pronunciation and *emphasis*.

☐ **THIS** is a great speech communication book. (As

124

Unintentional Messages Without Words Experiment

Goal: To demonstrate that as human beings we are transmitters and therefore we cannot help but communicate!

Step 1: Your instructor will assign you a partner or you can pick someone you don't know and find a space to yourselves.

Step 2: Making sure you are not touching each other, sit back to back with your partner. For this step, do not look at each other (this is very important).

Step 3: Next you and your partner should talk for two minutes about whatever subject you choose.

Step 4: Now turn around so that you're facing your partner, seated at a comfortable distance. Continue to carry on your conversation so that you can both see and hear each other for an additional two minutes.

Step 5: Next face your partner, but for the next two minutes hold your partner's hands and refrain from speaking. Send unspoken messages back and forth using sight and touch only. Make sure you are aware of any feelings you may experience during this phase of the experiment. There is no right way to behave here—there's nothing wrong with feeling silly or embarrassed. The main focus in this step is that *you must remain silent*.

After completing the last phase of this experiment, share your feelings during each step of the experiment. Share with each other honest feelings and perceptions about the *messages sent without words*. Were some of these messages without words perceived as uncomfortableness, nervousness, playfulness, silliness, or affectionate feelings? Could your partner tell these feelings without you expressing them? If so, how did this happen? Did you notice hand perspiration, lack of eye contact in your friend or any other messages without words that told you something?

opposed to some other speech communication book.)

☐ This is a **GREAT** speech communication book. (This book is superior!)

☐ This is a great **SPEECH** communication book. (This book is good as far as speech goes; it may not be so great as far as mass communication goes.)

☐ This is a great speech communication **BOOK**. (The text in question is not a record, novel, or play; it's a book.)

Paralanguage

The voice also sends messages through speed, tone, pitch, number and length of pauses, stammering, use of uh, um, er, volume, and so on. Researchers have identified six basic emotions that facial expressions reflect: sadness, fear, surprise, anger, disgust, and happiness (Ekman and Friesen). These expressions reflect these feelings and are recognizable in all cultures worldwide. The way that you say words identifies the emotion being expressed as well as the intensity of the statement. For example, in sarcasm both emphasis and tone of voice can change a statement's meaning to the opposite of the verbal message. Try the "Paralanguage Experiment."

Paralanguage Experiment

Goal: To show that voice tone and emphasis change a statements meaning.

Step 1: State each statement below literally.

Step 2: State each statement below with sarcasm.

"Honey, what a beautiful little dress!"

"She has to carry a heavy burden."

"I don't want to disgrace you!"

Note: Researchers have found that when vocal factors (tone, sarcasm, and emphasis) contradict the "words," the majority of people perceive the vocal factors as the more believable.

The Three Major Nonverbal Message Groups

Three major nonverbal concepts relevant to oral communication are **Proxemics, Indicators, and Kinesics.**

Proxemics

We all need our personal "space." When we determine or establish physical boundaries relevant to another person's location, we communicate something. There is a "bubble" around each of us. Humans take space very seriously.

Signs declaring "No Trespassing," "Keep Out," or "Private Property" declare underlying personal feelings or interpersonal behavior norms. As an effective communicator you should understand the

Proxemics Experiment

Goal: To demonstrate that the distance you allow between your self and someone else sends unspoken messages about you.

Step 1: Choose a partner.

Step 2: Begin talking to your partner and slowly inch closer, then a little closer and observe the other person's behavior.

Step 3: Each participant should be keenly aware of his/her perceptions and feelings during this experiment.

Step 4: Next, discuss with your partner how s/he felt as you moved closer in each other's proxemics zones.

Also note that the behavioral response for the opposite sex is much different than for members of the same sex moving closer. Obviously, you will be perceived as making a much different nonverbal statement by moving closer to a member of the same sex than to a member of the opposite sex.

principles of proxemics and how its use or avoidance can help you communicate better. How do you feel in a crowded situation? Try the "Proxemics Experiment" to determine how you really feel about your personal space.

Proxemics is the study of how you use space to communicate. It is a large field of study all to itself. For our purposes, one of the most useful insights comes from Edward Hall's work in communication distances or "comfort zones."

The term "proxemics" is from the Greek word "to approach" and refers to the analysis of body locations. The four proxemic zones are:

- **skin to 2 ft.—intimate**
- **2 to 4 ft.—personal**
- **4 to 7 ft.—social**
- **10 to . . .—public**

Hall actually broke these zones down further, which accounts for some of the variations in the numbers. He also pointed out that many factors lead to variations. The important point is not the specific numbers associated with the distances, but rather that our use of space is very much a part of our communication, and the way we treat it tells something about the relationship between the speaker and the listener.

For instance, a salesperson may discreetly move closer to a prospect after conversing for some time at a social distance. If the prospect allows the salesperson to remain at the closer distance, it indicates some level of trust has been established. If the prospect unconsciously takes a step back to re-establish social distance, there may still be some trust-building to do.

Proxemic zones are fairly highly-defined on the North American continent. However, proxemic zones may vary from society to society and among different cultures.

As discussed earlier, nonverbal communication is culture-bound.

For example, people from the Middle East and Northern Europe conduct routine business and converse publicly at a much closer distance than those on the North American continent. So, an individual from America may feel uncomfortable conversing with an individual from the Middle East and not quite know why, and *vice versa.* Being aware of proxemics in human interaction may help you be a better communicator.

"Space" may also refer to a person's location, status and authority, or the space that an individual takes or fills. Social scientists have determined that the space we fill makes the following statements:

Height
- Symbol of power and superiority
- Put upon a pedestal
- Look up to
- On top of the world
- Up to it

Lack of height
- Symbol of inferiority
- Fall short
- Think Small
- Short sighted
- Look down on

Indicators

The objects in our possession transmit clear messages about us. The clothes we wear and our furniture, paintings, and home are all explicit indicators of our behavior and status and are all nonverbal statements. For

128

example, a wedding ring says we're married. A ring on the right hand may suggest we're available. A police badge asserts authority and a particular uniform may announce a person's occupation.

Indicators (a sociological term) are objects we gather or our personal style we choose, such as in home furnishings, clothes, and hair styles.

Clothing

Although clothing covers our nakedness and protects us from the elements, communication theorist agree that clothing is also a very important means of sending "messages without words." Clothing conveys several types of messages to your fellow human beings. These messages may be stereotypical in nature and may vary from culture to culture, but nonetheless clothing nonverbally communicates something about you. Some of the general messages conveyed by clothing are
√ Economic level
√ Educational level
√ Trustworthiness
√ Social position
√ Level of sophistication
√ Economic background
√ Social background
√ Educational background
√ Level of success
√ Moral character

Brainstorm for a minute and honestly write what each of the above concepts might look like, as represented by various types of clothing.

What do clothes indicate? Does a waitress uniform or service uniform indicate a nonperson (not that we believe people in these positions *are* nonpersons, but rather that it is much easier to treat people wearing uniforms as functions rather than people)? Other clothing may nonverbally imply a sporty, feminine, sloppy, neat, or youthful person.

Clothing Research Findings

Research indicates that we do make stereotypical assumptions about people based on our own personal biases. For example one researcher studied males and females that were stationed in a hallway so that anyone who walked by had to avoid them or pass between them. Passers-by walked closer to the well-dressed couple and walked farther away from the same couple that was dressed casually or dressed as homeless persons. In another study pedestrians were more likely to follow a high-status dresser across a crosswalk even if the "don't walk" sign was flashing. The assumption that is made here is that people are more likely to follow the lead of high-status dressers, when it comes to violating social laws or norms (Molloy).

For your assigned speeches, for professional speaking, or for job interviews certain guidelines can be used for "dressing the part." Your speech instructor may encourage you to dress up or "dress the part" for your presentations. Dressing the part is effective nonverbal language. Remember, you are your own best visual aid.

Depending on the occasion, you may choose to vary from suggested attire. For example, the "power suit" may not be appropriate attire if you suspect your prospective employer or your audience may be easily intimidated by an assertive, well-dressed person. As a rule, dress as you imagine most of your audience will be dressed.

Kinesics

You may have noticed that some people seem to be easier to understand or communicate with. Such people may have more pronounced body language, or you may be more skillful than others at accurately encoding nonverbal behavior. Such study of behavior is called **kinesics**.

Kinesics is defined as the study and skillful interpretation of body language. Body language is defined as the study of perceptions of each physical movement that each body part makes.

Have you ever noticed an individual who walks with his/her shoulders slumped or who will not look you in the eye? What do these nonverbal signs and symbols mean? The study of such behavior is kinesics, or the analysis of physical movements.

Warning: If you take these behavioral symbols out of context, you may make a mistake. No single nonverbal communication sign can be read accurately out of context of the entire communication process. For example, an individual who crosses his/her arms on the chest after being told, "I don't like the way you dress!" would be communicating defensiveness.

Kinesic Communication Includes:
- √ crossing your arms
- √ a red face
- √ shaking your fist at someone
- √ giving the OK hand gesture
- √ pointing index finger
- √ sideways glance
- √ a cold hard lump of nothing in your throat
- √ hand covering your mouth while speaking
- √ pulling away
- √ biting your finger nails
- √ not looking at the other person

On the other hand, an individual who has arms crossed on the chest after you say "hello" would probably not be communicating defensiveness at all, but may just need to get comfortable.

All nonverbal cues need to be interpreted in the context of the entire communication. This would include verbal language, paralanguage (laughing, coughing, throat clearing, vocal pitch, and pauses,) and nonverbal

131

communication including proxemics, indicators, and kinesics.

By being conscious of these nonverbal communication concepts and how to interpret them, you will help yourself better understand interpersonal relationships and the communication process generally.

Attitudes Nonverbally Communicated by Physical Movements

Openness
Open hands
Unbuttoned coat
Defensiveness
Arms crossed on chest
Legs crossed
Fistlike gestures
Pointed index finger

Evaluation
Hand-to-face gestures
Head tilted
Stroking chin
Peering over glasses
Pipe smoker gestures

Suspicion
Arms crossed
Sideways glance
Touching or rubbing
   nose/eyes
Buttoning coat
Drawing away

Insecurity
Pinching flesh
Chewing pen, pencil
Rubbing thumb over
   thumb
Biting fingernails
Hands in pockets

Nervousness	*Cooperation*
Clearing throat	Upper body in sprinter's position
"Whew" sound	
Whistling	Open hands
Fidgeting in chair	Sitting on edge of chair
Hand covering mouth while speaking	Hand-to-face gestures
	Tilted head
Not looking at other person	Unbuttoning coat
Jingling money in pockets	
Tugging at ear	
Perspiration	

Study questions

Why is nonverbal communication important to a speaker?

What are some of the ways we communicate nonverbally?

What does "proxemics" refer to, and why does it matter to a speaker on a platform?

Works Cited in Chapter

Birdwhistle, Ray. *Kinesics and Context*. Philadelphia: University of Pennsylvania Press, 1970.

Ekman, Paul, and Wallace V. Friesen. *Unmasking the Face: A Guide to Recognizing Emotions from Facial Clues*. Englewood Cliffs, N.J.: Prentice-Hall, 1975.

Hall, Edward T. *Beyond Culture*. Garden City, N.Y.: Anchor Books, 1977.

Hall, Edward T. *The Silent Language*. New York: Doubleday, 1959.

Lapakko, David. "Three Cheers for Language: A Closer Examination of a Widely Cited Study of Nonverbal Communication." *Communication Education 46* (1997).

Mehrabian, Albert. *Nonverbal Communication*. Chicago: Aldine-Atherton, 1972.

Mehrabian, Albert. *Silent Messages*. Belmont, CA: Wadsworth, 1971.

Molloy, John T. *John T. Molloy's New Dress for Success*. New York: Warner Books, 1988.

Monroe, Alan H. "Measurement and Analysis of Audience Reaction to Student Speakers' Studies in Attitude Changes." *Bulletin of Purdue University Studies in Higher Education 22* (1937).

Wood, Barbara S. *Messages Without Words*. New York: Raintree Steck-Vaughn Publishers, 1988.

Chapter 13

Delivery: Mechanics of Presenting to an Audience

There are four modes of delivery for public speaking, each of which has advantages and disadvantages. Let's examine a chart that will compare them, and talk about the situations in which you would use each.

See Figure 13.1 for a chart that shows the relationship of these modes.

Manuscript

As we have said in class, people don't write the way they talk, so when you prepare a speech by writing a manuscript, it is likely to sound written instead of "spoken." However, there are situations in which its advantages outweigh its disadvantages. For instance, if you happen to be the president of the United States and will deliver a speech at a press conference (in other words, your exact wording is going to be scrutinized and picked apart), then getting the words exactly right will be more important than having good eye contact.

In such a situation, manuscript mode also gives you the opportunity to hand out copies of your manuscript, which helps make sure you are quoted accurately. Plus, you can actually have someone else, or even a team of others, write the speech for you. This means your time can be spent on other things. Your delivery still may sound wooden, but people sort of expect that in a formal speech.

Memorized

You can also have someone else write the speech in

Mode	Nature	Advantages/ Disadvantages
Manuscript	Written out word for word	• Sounds wooden • Sounds written • Lots of preparation time • Interferes with eye contact • Can't vary from it easily • Can polish the exact wording
Memorized	Memorized word for word	• All the same as Manuscript, plus: • Danger of forgetting • Extra stress, knowing you're working "without a net" • Useful if speech will be delivered several times
Impromptu	Only a couple of minutes to prepare	• Can't check out facts • Tend to ramble • Hard to control time • *May* lead to high anxiety • Sounds very spontaneous, conversational • *May* lessen anxiety—no time to get nervous
Extemporaneous	Speaking from notes	• Time to prepare organization • Time to research • Word choice leads to spontaneous, oral sound • Takes some preparation, not as much as Manuscript and Memorizing • Extremely adaptable

Figure 13.1: Modes of Delivery and their relative advantages and disadvantages.

memorized delivery. In addition, your hands are freed, so in theory your gestures and other nonverbal communication could be very good. However, in practice you may be so worried about forgetting your speech that you forget to move, losing the advantage.

As the chart notes, this delivery mode is particularly useful if you will deliver the exact same speech several times. For instance, if you are going to deliver the same sales pitch over and over, memorizing it allows you to "amortize" the time you spend writing and memorizing the speech. In other words, if you spend three hours writing and four hours memorizing a 15-minute speech delivered one time, you have a huge investment of preparation. But if you deliver the same 15-minute speech 10 times a day, five days a week, the three hours writing and four hours memorizing is a good investment.

Impromptu

Impromptu delivery is almost a separate skill, the ability to think on your feet. Although most people use it to mean speaking with no preparation whatsoever, the technical term means that you speak with very little preparation. Usually you have about five minutes or so to collect your thoughts.

When would you use this? In any situation in which you will not have time to prepare. For instance, that certain someone you have wanted to ask out sits down at your table in the cafeteria. Act now or lose the opportunity. Or, you're at a club meeting and something that wasn't on the agenda comes up. If you don't speak up now, something you dislike very much will happen. Think briefly, marshal your thoughts, jot a couple of very brief notes, and then make your point.

Extemporaneous

This is the workhorse of public speaking. You prepare, you have your facts together, you are ready, and yet you don't sound like a machine. It is the compromise between extremes for most of the delivery issues we have discussed. For instance, your eye contact cannot be as good as with impromptu, but it will be much better than with manuscript.

The preparation of a full-sentence outline should be much different than the preparation of a manuscript. Your outline is a record of the relationship among ideas. When you put your speaking notes together, the ideas may be *revealed* in a different order. And since your speaking notes consist of one or two words to *remind* you of each point, the way you say the points will be much more conversational than if you were reading them or memorizing them word for word.

> **Extemporaneous delivery will work for you 80 percent of the time.**

Extemporaneous delivery will work for you 80 percent of the time. Don't burden yourself with the preparation time and delivery drawbacks of memorized or manuscripted delivery unless the specific situation calls for their advantages. Take it easy on yourself, and use extemporaneous.

By the way, even if you know your speech cold, and think you don't need notes, take them up there with you anyway. You don't have to *look* at them. But just knowing they're there if you need them gives you the same peace of mind that a pilot has knowing that the parachute is available should the need arise.

Practical Application of Extemporaneous

When you read about extemporaneous speaking, you learned that, contrary to popular opinion, it is not the same as impromptu. When you speak extemporaneously, you prepare your research, your organization, your points ahead of time. You just don't work out your exact wording. You don't write out your speech word for word. You certainly don't memorize it.

Just to be clear and for emphasis, let's state: **Do not write your speech out word for word.** You should *only* prepare notes. People don't talk the way they write. A manuscript interferes with eye contact. Don't.

Because of that, the working definition for extemporaneous speaking could be "speaking from notes." Earlier we distinguished between your preparation outline and your notes. We said then that a preparation outline is a "map" of the relationship of ideas; it is not necessarily your order of presentation. To work most confidently and effectively, you should take your preparation outline and from it make a set of notes that will a) remind you of your order of presentation, and b) work for you. There is no one "correct" way to make speaking notes. But based on the experience of hundreds of others, we can make suggestions that have a high probability of working for you.

Some concerns

People often worry that without a manuscript they will forget what they want to say. As we discussed earlier in the section on modes of delivery, there are times when the manuscript or memorized mode of delivery works better than extemporaneous, but those times are relatively rare. In most of the situations in which we will speak, extemporaneous delivery actually makes you more comfortable in front of an audience, because it's more natural.

When you read from a manuscript, the psychological emphasis becomes saying the words exactly as you prepared them. If you stumble over a word, or get a couple out of order, you will inevitably back up, bumble a little, and repeat the phrases as necessary in order to get them just as they are on paper.

When you speak extemporaneously, the psychological emphasis is on getting your ideas across. You are much freer to respond to the audience, to change your wording or choose different examples or whatever you have to do to get the point across. Paradoxically, you are less likely to stumble over your words because you're not trying to create a perfect reproduction of what you rehearsed. You speak more smoothly and confidently, because it is much more like what you do every single day of your life—talk with people in a conversational manner.

Extemporaneous speaking is not exactly like conversation, of course, because you seldom have your research and your organization all worked out before a conversation. An extemporaneous speech goes much more smoothly than the typical conversation. Think of it this way: Almost all of us have experienced hindsight. After a conversation or an argument ends, then you think of the brilliant reply or comeback. "If only I could have thought faster," you say to yourself, "I could have really nailed that point."

Extemporaneous delivery is what a conversation would sound like if you had the chance to prepare your thoughts ahead of time, if you could actually turn back time and take advantage of hindsight. It's a great opportunity!

Don't worry about forgetting what the notes mean. You won't, because they are your notes. Compare effective speaking notes to an effective shopping list. When I go to

Wal-Mart, I make a list first so I don't forget anything. But the list reminds me of what I thought in the first place, so it doesn't have to be extensive. When I see "TP" on my list, I not only remember that it stands for toilet paper, I also remember what brand and how many plies and how many rolls are supposed to be in a pack. It works because it's my list.

But if Janet (my wife) makes the list for me and just hands it to me, I won't know all that when I see "TP" on the list. Maybe I'll figure it stands for toilet paper, but I may be very wrong on all the other stuff. It will be especially disconcerting if, when I get home, I find she meant for me to get toothpaste.

By the same token, if you tried to work from somebody else's speaking notes, you might very well stumble around a lot and go in the wrong direction. But that won't happen to you, because they are your notes prepared from your thoughts and your outline.

As we discussed when we talked about outline mechanics in Chapter 9, think of the difference between your favorite song as performed by your favorite band and what that song looks like reduced to paper. Some of you read music; others may be familiar with "guitar tabs." Surely no one thinks that what's on the paper is the song! It represents the song, and helps the musician perform the song, but it's not the song. In a similar way, your notes only remind you of what you want to say; they are not, themselves, the speech, and there is nothing sacred about them (in other words, you have permission to vary from them; they're not written in stone, they're written on biodegradable note cards).

With that in mind, let's look at some helpful suggestions for making them work better for you.

The Suggestions

Keep your notes to a minimum. As a general rule, the fewer the notes the better. As a comparison, here is a brief reproduction of a portion of a sample outline:

Figure 13.1: Sample portion of a preparation outline.

> I. Carat, the first C, is the weight of the diamond.
>   A. Diamond weight has only recently been standardized.
>   1. Originally merchants measured diamonds against the seed of the cabob.
>   2. Now the carat has been standardized as 200 milligrams.

The speech as delivered sounded something like this:

Carat, the first C, is a measure of the weight of the diamond. Diamond merchants in the middle east first began to weigh diamonds using a weight-and-balance system like you may have used in a chemistry lab, the kind where you place what you want to weigh on one side and then put standardized weights on the other side until it is nearly perfectly balanced. But instead of using those chemistry lab weights, diamond merchants would drop the seeds of the cabob plant on the side that balanced the diamond. The problem, of

142

course, was that seeds with different moisture content or from a different crop might weigh more or less, so what was a 3 carat diamond last year might be a 2 1/2 carat diamond this year. So eventually diamond merchants settle on a standard of 200 milligrams to a carat.

You can see from this that the speech as delivered had quite a bit more verbiage than the outline. The speaking notes, though, showed a differential as well. They looked something like figure 13.2.

Figure 13.2: Sample portion of speaking notes.

Carat
Cabob
200 mg

If someone just picked up that card, he would be mystified. But the notes made sense to the person who wrote them and who just needed a reminder of what to say.

The fact is, if you only include a few words, you spend less time studying them and more time looking at (and, more importantly, *connecting with*) the audience.

Use cardboard or stiff paper. Lots of people use notebook or legal pad paper. More and more people produce notes from a computer. But that can lead people to make speaking notes on regular paper, which causes several practical problems.

Regular sheets of paper stick together, especially under high humidity conditions. Regular paper gets blown off the lectern easily, or slides under the lip of the lectern to the floor. Regular paper is harder to handle. It's mainly available in 8 1/2 by 11 size, which is awkward to handle—you either fold it up or roll it up, and then it won't lay flat on the lectern.

It's just better to use heavier weight stock. At the least, get card-weight stock to run through your printer. Better: use a template in Word or Wordperfect to put your notes into card-sized blocks, then print it on card weight stock and cut it apart.

A professor we know used to print his notes out on regular paper, then cut the paper up and paste it to 5 x 7 note cards.

For those of you who don't use computers to print notes (and even for those who do), consider using a manila folder for your notes. Not to *hold* your notes, but for your actual notes. Write on the folder. It's like having four sheets of 8 1/2 by 11 paper, but they can't get separated and can't get out of order. You can put any transparencies or handouts right in the folder and be certain that you have all your materials for the speech in one place.

Finally, there's just the old-fashioned way of handwriting on index cards. It works! Experiment with different sizes—try 4 x 6 and 5 x 7 note cards, and you may find they work better than 3 x 5.

Design your notes for accessibility. Make it easy to use your notes. This leads to a lot of practical advice by way of example—take the time to think of more practical considerations. Here are a few ideas:

- Print instead of using cursive.
- Write in big, easy-to-see letters. You should be able to easily read them from two feet away. Don't try to cram every little thing onto a note card just so you can say you used note cards instead of full sheets of paper.
- Use different colors of ink to represent main points, statistics, stories, etc. That way if you get lost you can immediately find your place.

144

- Use only one side of the note cards.
- Number your note cards so that you can get them back in order quickly if you drop them.
- If you feel compelled to write on both sides of the note card, number fronts and backs in different corners, so that you can quickly not only get them in order but all face up.
- Turn the note card vertically (like a piece of paper) instead of horizontally (like a recipe card).

Make meta-notes. This means to make notes about your notes. Think of notes as being like dialogue in a play script, and meta-notes as being stage directions. These are things that would likely *not* show up in your preparation outline, but would need to be done during the speech.

Make the metanotes visually different so you don't confuse them with notes—otherwise, you might end up saying your "stage directions" out loud! Use a different color ink, or set them at an angle. Since I print my notes out on computer, I use handwriting for the metanotes. You can even use pictures if you are a visual thinker.

Metanotes can be things you want to do, notations about the page number of a quotation in a book, or even reminders about more general behaviors. For instance, I once had a student who had a fairly wooden style of delivery who put little smiley faces at various places in the notes as a visual reminder to smile at her audience.

Use visual materials as notes. Many times audiences believe that speakers go through an entire four-hour seminar with no notes, because they don't see him or her holding notes. Actually, the speaker has notes in front of everybody for all the world to see—if she's using PowerPoint or transparencies to put the points into bullet format. With a glance at the screen, the speaker gets a reminder of what she wants to say.

This approach doesn't think of notes as necessarily words. You had to structure your speech to prepare your visual aids, so the visual aids can work as a reminder of your planned speech. If you have a guitar that you're going to use to demonstrate something about changing strings, the object itself will remind you of what to say next.

Paralanguage (Vocal) Concerns

Speak Up and Slow Down

A speech that is not heard cannot be effective. Check with audience members to make sure they can hear you.

The normal rate of speaking is around 140 words per minute, but under pressure we tend to speak faster. Because of the adrenaline, when you seem to yourself to be speaking slowly, you're probably speaking at a normal rate.

Also remember that the larger the audience is, the slower you have to speak. You have to account for floor noise, poor lighting, and other distractions. Plus, since your audience can't *see* you nearly as well, they will miss a lot of the nonverbal cues we take for granted in conversation. Just don't confuse speaking more slowly with speaking more flatly. Slow your rate, but keep your *energy* high.

Natural Pitch

Speak at your natural pitch. You may have to experiment to find out what your natural pitch is. Here's a "trick" to keep it natural. Pretend you are holding a glass of water up to your lips, about to take a drink. Just before taking the first swallow, stop and note how relaxed and open your throat feels. Pay attention to the physical feeling. If you can reproduce that feeling as you begin talking, you are likely to be speaking at your natural pitch, as well as giving yourself the best opportunity for speaking up.

Vocal Intonation

Intonation, which includes vocal shifts and inflections, helps give emphasis to ideas. Rising intonation at the end of a sentence suggests a question, while a downward inflection is associated with a completed thought and helps emphasize an idea.

You can communicate subtle connotations by varying your voice in this fashion. Remember our demonstration in class. Saying "I did not *say* he beat his wife" indicates you didn't say it explicitly, although you may have implied it. Saying "I did not say *he* beat his wife" indicates that someone else may have beaten his wife.

Be Yourself

You are okay the way you are. Be your best self, but be yourself; don't try to imitate someone else. Don't compare yourself to anyone else; just compare yourself to yourself. Just let your concern for the subject matter and for the audience show.

Keep the Microphone Out of Your Mouth

The proper distance for a microphone can be found by spreading your fingers open as far as they will go. The distance from the tip of your thumb to the tip of your little finger is about the right distance. In addition, don't speak directly *into* the microphone; position it just above chest level, and then aim it at your mouth (it will be at about a 45 degree angle). Keep in mind most microphones accept sound within a cone-shaped area, and just keep your head within that cone.

Nonverbal Elements

Impression Formation

From the moment you first appear before your audience until you leave, you are forming impressions in the minds of your listeners. The confidence with which you approach the situation, the fact that you look directly at members of your audience, the determined but interested look on your face, and the ease with which you move all contribute to impression formation.

Most audiences will remember relatively little of the actual details you present to them, but they *will* carry away with them their impression of you.

Audience members need to feel that they are involved in an interaction with you. The way you behave is crucial to the way your audience responds. Remember, actions speak louder than words.

Facial and Vocal Cues

The mouth and eyebrows signal pleasant and unpleasant emotions. The eyes and mouth together are the most reliable indicators of a speaker's emotional state.

Several studies, as reported by Michael Hanna and James Gibson, show that listeners can accurately detect anger from the tone of your voice two-thirds of the time. A great deal can be communicated just by the sound of your voice.

Body Movements

1. *Stand quietly or move for a reason.* Plan your general movements. If you want to make a point by moving, do so. However, have a reason for the movement or stand still.

2. *Use gestures naturally.* Animation helps you communicate more effectively. Gestures involve the movement of hands, arms, or head to reinforce what you are saying. Gestures should be natural, emphatic enough to be noticed, and consistent with your words. Don't overpractice; let gestures flow naturally from what you are saying.

3. *Stand beside your visual aids, not in front of them.* Undoubtedly, you have seen a speaker turn his or her back to an audience to write on a chalkboard, then position himself between the audience and what he just wrote. Stand beside the visuals as you refer to them, then put them away and move once again toward your audience (more about visual aids in another handout).

4. *Don't fidget.* Avoid distracting your audience by displaying random gestures and awkward posture. Avoid scratching, plucking at loose threads, adjusting your clothes, or brushing dandruff from your shoulders. Do not comb your hair (don't laugh, it has happened in our classes!)

Study questions

1. How do extemporaneous and impromptu speeches differ?

2. What should you do to make speaking notes effective?

3. What do most people need to do with their voices to be effective at delivering a speech?

Works Cited in Chapter

Hanna, Michael S., and James W. Gibson. *Public Speaking for Personal Success.* Needham Heights, Mass.: Pearson Custom Publishing, 1999.

Chapter 14

Informative Speeches

In Chapter 6 we looked briefly at the specific kinds of speeches. In this chapter we want to examine one of them more deeply: the instructive or informative speech.

Arguably, sharing information forms the basis of human society. We could go so far as to claim that sharing information is what makes humans human. The ability to preserve and share what we have learned in a highly structured way makes human progress possible. We even have a folk saying about "not reinventing the wheel," which advises us to take advantage of the learning that others have already done. If it were not for the ability to share information, we would each literally have to reinvent the wheel for ourselves.

> **Sharing information forms the basis of human society.**

Informing is also the basis for other types of speaking. You can't persuade someone unless you can first inform him.

Beyond Mere Facts

We use the term "information" somewhat loosely. We simply mean helping your audience understand something as you understand it. It's not about convincing them that you're right, but letting them see from your viewpoint. In pursuit of that, you will share factual information, but also opinions, perceptions, ideas, and perhaps even outlandish notions. All of this falls under the heading of "informing."

Emphasis on Understanding

Once a college roommate of mine (Wes) was sitting on his bed in the dorm eating sardines out of a can balanced precariously on his knee. He had that nasty sardine juice slathered all the way up to both elbows. A dog wandered into the room (yes, it was *that* kind of dorm) and sidled tentatively up to him, sniffing longingly at the can.

Wes said, "Don't you touch them sardines!"

The dog, of course, kept coming closer.

"I said, 'Don't you touch them!'"

The dog poked his nose directly into the can and tipped it onto the floor, at which point Wes soundly thumped the dog between the eyes. The dog yelped and ran out of the room with his tail tucked.

My other roommate (Parris) said, "Wes, man, that was mean. Why did you hit that dog?"

Wes looked completely confused and said, "I warned him! I mean, I *told* him not to touch the sardines!"

Simply saying something does little good. Since all communication is audience-centered, make the effort to check whether your audience members understand what you say to them.

Basics of Informing

Here, then are some thoughts on effectively helping audiences to understanding what you're trying to get across to them.

Make Sure the Ideas Are Clear

Refer back to Chapter 6 on selecting specific purposes, and to Chapters 8 and 9 on organizing and outlining. Those skills will help you inform the audience by helping you to get clear with yourself what ideas you want the audience to get from the speech. Too many speakers actually start speaking with no more in mind than "I'm going to do a speech about skiing." That's only a general topic. You may have detailed notes, but oral details without structure will simply overwhelm an audience.

Although it is an oversimplification, it's useful to differentiate the kind of information people understand most easily according to how they get the information. "Out loud" (i.e., spoken) is better for presenting the "big picture," setting context, and explaining patterns and relationships among ideas. "In print" (i.e., words, pictures, bullet lists) is better for mastering details.

So spend some time thinking about the major ideas you want them to retain, then use the specific details of your speech to make those ideas understandable and memorable.

Figure 14.1: Approaches to choosing a specific topic from a general topic area.

Topic area

Appeal to Their Self-interest

Audience members care about what matters to audience members. This tautology is often overlooked even by experienced speakers, who may believe the audience will be interested in a topic simply because the speaker is. Look at your topic from *their* point of view. Why should they care?

Avoid Information Overload

Don't bury them with your information. You may have spent hours researching your topic, and you only have 10 minutes to present it. It's tempting to just try to hit the high points and summarize what you've found—but

153

that usually bores the audience. (I once had a student try to do a five-minute speech on the history of the United States. World War II would have been reduced to "it was bad"!) You can either go for broad and shallow, or narrow and deep (see Figure 14.1). Take our advice: go for the narrow and deep. Select a "vertical" slice of your topic area that is narrow enough for you to handle in the time allotted and deep enough for you to hold audience members' interest.

Use Signposting

Signposting simply tells the audience members where you are in your journey with them. It works the same way taking a trip does. Before you leave, you probably look at a map and figure out that you'll need to drive to Nashville on Interstate 40, for instance, get on Interstate 65, and go north to get where you want to go. Along the way you look for signs that tell you if you're on the right road or not. Even though you think you're on the right road, it makes you feel on track when you see those little I-40 West signs.

In your introduction tell your audience what you intend to do. "Today we'll discuss three ways to cook chicken." During your speech, say things like, "The first way we'll discuss is…."

You'll also want to pay attention to transitions. They help the audience know when you're moving from one point to another, and to stay with you.

Use Supporting Material to Accomplish Your Tasks

Go back and look at Chapter 10. Don't forget to include both hard supporting material that proves and establishes your point and appeal to logos (you need to convince the audience you know what you're talking about, even in an informative speech) *and* soft supporting material that clarifies and explains your point.

Use Repetition and Multiple Channels

When a reader doesn't understand something, she can go back over it and read it again. When a listener doesn't understand something you've said, she's just lost. One of the major differences in communicating via written and spoken channels is the need to go back over material (in interesting ways) to help listeners "get it." Don't repeat word-for-word, but find different ways to present the information again. "Present again" may mean via the same channel (such as giving a principle and then giving an example, both of which utilize spoken words) or via a parallel channel (such as showing a visual aid (see Chapter 17) while explaining it).

Summary

It's not rocket science, but informing is a skill that takes conscious thought to develop. Don't treat it as simply a "paper out loud." Through the application of these and other principles and guidelines, you can effectively share the understanding you have with other people.

Study questions
1. Why is informative speaking such an important activity?
2. How can you focus your information before presenting it to your audience?
3. What is signposting?

Chapter 15

Persuasive Speeches

Persuasion is the attempt to change or reinforce an attitude, belief, or behavior. It is a huge field of study all by itself, but with a little thought and understanding of the process, you can improve your ability to influence other people.

By the way, we're not talking about coercion (changing behavior by force) or deceit, which many people seem to equate with persuasion. Because we're talking about genuine communication, which implies a respect between the communicators (both coercion and deceit requires treating the other person as an object), persuasion in turn implies a respect for and an understanding of the recipient of the persuasive attempt. When practiced properly and ethically, persuasion benefits both the persuader and the person being persuaded—even if the person being persuaded ultimately decides against the course of action being urged.

> **Persuasion benefits both the persuader and the person being persuaded.**

Assume, for instance, that you work in sales, selling a product you believe in (i.e., you believe it actually serves the needs of your customers). Let's say that you sell a particular brand of car. Because you believe your success in sales depends on building relationships, getting referrals, and getting repeat business, you spend some time getting to know a prospect and finding out what her transportation needs are, as well as her financial situation. If you have accurately assessed her situation, and your product really does solve her transportation problems (including fitting within her budget), then does she win or lose if you succeed in persuading her to buy a car from you?

Let's be clear that we do not approach persuasion as a zero-sum game in which the other person loses when you win.

Persuasion is the attempt to change or reinforce an attitude, belief, or behavior. It involves whatever techniques are used by a person to influence the thoughts and/or behavior of other people. In fact, throughout our lives other people influence our actions and beliefs directly or indirectly by using their persuasive skills (intentionally or unintentionally) to appeal to our individual physiological and psychological motivations.

Why have you chosen to attend this school? You may answer that it satisfies your needs and will help you achieve your personal goals. But how did you learn that this school offers what you are looking for? Perhaps you found out from friends, relatives, the media, or a school representative who recruited you. In other words, your decision to enroll was based both on the persuasive skills of others and on your personal goals. When you realize and understand the means by which you are convinced to accept an idea or perform an action, you can deliberately use these same strategies to influence others to fund your project proposal, to manufacture your invention, to change a procedure, or even to hire you.

When you intend to influence the thoughts or actions of your audience in an oral presentation, first consider the actual purpose of your talk and identify your audience.

Purpose

Before you begin planning an effective persuasive talk, you need to determine precisely the outcome you seek in terms of audience response.

Do you want the audience members to open their minds to your thoughts (make inroads), to alter their way of thinking or of doing something (simple persuasion), or to make a physical commitment to their beliefs (actuate). Do you hope to change a conviction or belief they now hold or to convince them to accept your belief as true? Or do you simply want to reinforce a belief they already have or to encourage them to continue what they're already doing? Probably no single plan of action will sway any one listener, but a combination or variety of strategies will likely reach most of them.

You are more likely to persuade an audience when your specific goal is clearly defined. One helpful way of thinking about your purpose classifies your specific purpose statement according to type of subject matter.

Audience Beliefs about Statements of Fact

These statements concern audience beliefs about the factualness of what is being asserted. On the surface, such speeches may appear to be informative speeches, but they are persuasive (speeches to convince) in that there is an element of doubt about the truthfulness of the proposition. Examples include:
- "I want the jury to believe that Simpson is guilty of murder."
- "I want my audience to believe that the Greenhouse effect is a reality."

Achieving one's purpose comes primarily from amassing evidence.

Audience Beliefs about Statements of Value

These specific purpose statements involve some sort of comparison. Thus, the standard of measurement must be included. Key words include words such as "better," "best," "more," "more valuable," and other similar comparison words. For instance, if you assert, "*The New York Times* is a better newspaper than *USA Today*," you will need to define what you mean by "better newspaper." If you mean "complete coverage, depth reporting, analysis, background," then the *Times* is better. If you mean "easy to read, predictable format, capsule format, coverage of entire country, can be read over breakfast," then *USA Today* probably wins.

Since comparisons and agreements form the heart of this type, these statements also lead to speeches to convince. Examples of value statements include:

- "I want my audience to believe that small schools are better for most students than large schools."
- "I want my audience to believe that Jones is the best quarterback in the league."

Audience Beliefs or Actions about Statements of Policy

Since these types of specific purpose statements deal either with audience beliefs or actions, they can form the basis of speeches to convince or actuate. Key words include words such as "should," "ought," "would be better to," and infinitives that lead to action. Often the difference between a speech to convince and a speech to actuate lies in whether the audience can actually do what is being advocated. For instance, the first example below is a speech to convince, since the audience does not possess the power to halt work on nuclear power plants (unless the audience happens to be members of the Department of Energy, the board of the Tennessee Valley Authority, or some similar agency). To make it a speech to actuate, edit it so that it includes something the audience can actually do, as in the second example.

160

- "I want the audience to believe that work on nuclear power plants should be halted."
- "I want the audience to sign a petition addressed to Congress urging that work on nuclear power plants be halted."
- "I want my audience to vote for an increased budget for women's athletics."

Audience Demographics

Persuasion, more than any other purpose for speaking, is based on audience response. You must know as much as possible about the characteristics of your audience (audience demographics) before you decide on your persuasive plan of attack.

You are more likely to persuade an audience when your specific goal is clearly defined.

The more you know about your audience members, the better chance you have of influencing them to respond as you hope.

For example, you may need to know what procedure they currently use and why, what beliefs they now hold and why, and what individual and organizational goals they have in order to convince them that your proposal is needed, is desirable, or is an improvement over what they now think and do.

Furthermore, your ideas may be more profitable, more logical, or may save time, space, money, or effort. You need to be as familiar as possible with the interests and objectives of your listeners so that you can emphasize how your suggestions can help them reach those objectives.

Demographics traditionally refer to such statistical information as average age, socioeconomic status, political affiliations, etc. Such statistics, like most statistics, must be interpreted correctly to be useful, but can give an indication about the audience.

Whether or not you take the statistical approach, seek to understand the audience in terms of the audience's interest in your subject, the audience's existing knowledge of your subject, and the audience's attitude toward your subject.

In other words, to take them where you believe they need to go, you have to start where they are.

Persuasive Strategies

Illustration by Todd Long

Although he is often called the "father of logic," Aristotle recognized that successful persuasion depends on more than logic alone. As humans, we are not logical; we are psychological.

Thus, Aristotle said that to succeed at persuasion, the speaker must establish credibility and appeal to both reasoning and emotions.

Establishing Credibility. In order for you to influence your audience they must believe you know what you are talking about (speaker *ethos*). You must have credibility; that is, you must be a believable, reliable source of information.

Research indicates that *ethos* comprises three independent but interwoven factors, all based on the audience's perception: your trustworthiness, your competence, and your likeability.

☐ **Trustworthiness** means that the audience believes you would not purposely do them harm—that you would not take advantage of them.

162

☐ **Competence** means that they believe you have done your homework and actually possess the capabilities and knowledge you claim.

☐ **Likeability** means that they like you, that they identify with you. It is no coincidence that in English we appear to have two different forms of the word "like" that are actually linguistically related. Someone might say, "I like you." Or he might say, "I am like you." Psychologically the two are closely related.

You can achieve credibility by making your experience, your knowledge, and your credentials known to your listeners; by delivering your speech confidently and enthusiastically; by using appropriate diction; and by maintaining a professional appearance. Most importantly you must research thoroughly and organize clearly.

Remember that persuasion is a skill (maybe even an art!) which you can develop, and that you can and should employ a variety of strategies and use whichever techniques are most likely to influence your audience.

Showing enthusiasm about your message and about the opportunity to "share" with your audience will also help you establish rapport (the "likeability" part) and, therefore, credibility with your audience. Enthusiasm is catching, and your presentation is more likely to stir your audience if your lively delivery demonstrates your enthusiasm and eagerness to communicate.

Appearance and credibility. Although the folk saying goes, "You can't tell a book by its cover," the fact remains that audience members have nothing **except** a "cover" to go by as they consider you. Why? They're not mind readers. Since they cannot **know** the "real you," they will only know what you present to them. You cannot escape the fact that in a professional context a neatly dressed, well-groomed individual gets a better reception. When you

163

meet expectations in this regard, your audience is more likely to hear you.

A business-like appearance will add to your credibility as a speaker. While it may be true that people should not be judged by the way they appear, you can take advantage of the reality that, at least to some extent, they are so judged! You are your own visual aid.

Aristotle defined *ethos* as the speaker's believability or credibility. It is established or re-established each time you get up to speak. It is not something you **have**; it is something the audience **perceives**. However, an understanding of it suggests some fairly simple steps you can take to influence it, steps with highly predictable results.

> **Ethos is not something you** have; **it is something the audience** perceives.

For instance, many people in our country know relatively little about political issues or the views of political candidates.

But because most candidates understand non-verbal communication and how to use it and have a command of human relations skills, they have become experts at creating an illusion of "high *ethos*." Right or wrong, they have learned to play the *ethos* game and create an illusion of believability.

Presenting Appeals

"Appeal" refers to a sincere entreaty or request or to a means of arousing interest. In job-related oral communication projects, it is more appropriate for you to arouse your audience's interest than to beg for compliance.

You cannot anticipate exactly what appeals will cause your audience to agree with you or to accept your suggestions; therefore, use a combination of rational appeals (*logos*) and emotional appeals (*pathos*) to encourage the listeners desirable response. Your appeals may be predominately rational or predominately emotional depending on the purpose of your talk, on the characteristics and motivations of your audience, and on your "product" itself.

Logos. Rational appeals may include the facts, statistics, evidence, or logic you use to prove or substantiate a persuasive argument. Most audiences cannot readily recognize formal arguments or test their validity, but they will react to whether your appeals "sound reasonable." The point is *not* to fool your audience; the point is to make sure your arguments *are* solid, and also *sound* solid.

To add to your credibility, distinguish clearly between what is **fact** and what is **opinion**. For example, "There is no human life on the earth's moon," is fact. "There is no human life on any planet other than Earth," is opinion. Facts are verifiable either by observation, by measurement, by demonstration, or by established truth. Opinion involves whatever someone believes to be true but which has not been proven. Make use of opinion, but make sure you do not try to pass it off as fact.

Although your opinions may be highly regarded by your listeners because you have established credibility, a specialized audience motivated by organizational goals will be more impressed by rational arguments. If and when you make a declarative statement, always back it up logically with evidence.

In our society, we believe "everyone is entitled to an opinion." That may be true, but if you want an audience to agree with you, you must do more than simply state opinion. Give the reasons behind the opinion, the evidence that supports the opinion, and then the audience can reasonably agree with it.

Pathos. Emotional appeals focus on the satisfaction of fundamental human needs, desires, and motivations, such as the need for food, shelter, clothing, safety and security, health, love, social interaction and acceptance, self-esteem, and self-actualization. To appeal to the sensibilities and emotion of your audience, you legitimately may use words with strongly positive or strongly negative connotations. However, since most professional talks will be given to technically knowledgeable audiences whose primary objectives are to meet the needs and requirements of the company or organization they represent, your efforts to arouse listeners' sensibilities would be supplementary or secondary to your logical and actual persuasive means. Be careful of demagoguery, particularly when working in a business or professional environment.

Nevertheless, to motivate people to action, you must appeal to their emotions. The word "emotion" comes from a Latin word which means "to move." The difference between being convinced (intellectual activity alone) and being actuated (behavior now involved) is often whether or not the emotions have been involved.

Using Sensory Devices

Attempting to affect your audience members by stimulating more than one of their five senses (sight, smell, touch, hearing, taste) can be a very persuasive technique. In fact, sometimes you can influence the listeners without their awareness of your deliberate manipulation—a technique common to advertising. For instance, the sight of a beautiful woman holding a bottle of cologne (itself an alluring shape and color) combined with the hearing of "emotional" words such as "sensuous," "alluring," and "seductive" can be very persuasive indeed! Add a pleasant fragrance and you've sold it!

Have you ever wondered why architectural models of proposed buildings always include sight-pleasing extras such as trees, grass, flowers, and people relaxing on park benches? They are definite and deliberate attempts to elicit a positive viewer reaction. Together with interest-arousing words such as "energy-efficient" (with statistics to prove it!), "state of the art." "sound construction," these visuals can obviously influence the outcome of an oral project proposal.

More importantly, people are more likely to remember what you say if they can see what you're talking about. Then you will have reached them through both their sense of hearing and their sense of sight. Visual aids can be the most powerful persuasive technique available to you, provided you use them wisely.

For instance, if you want to institute a peer evaluation system to increase production in your department, present a clearly visible line graph depicting productivity decline over the last year. At a glance your audience will be convinced that improvements are needed. Having aroused their interest then you are well on your way to persuading them that you have a feasible answer to the problem. Combined with other persuasive strategies, your visual aids can be extremely influential factor.

Combining Ethos, Logos, and Pathos

Keep the three modes of persuasion in balance for greatest effect.

Although logically the person presenting the information does not change the truth or falsehood of the information, psychologically it makes a great deal of difference as to whether the listener accepts the information. If certain politicians said the sun came up this

Mode	English words derived from	Meaning and implications in public speaking
Logos	Logic, Psychology	Appeal to reasoning; not necessarily formal logic; whether it "sounds reasonable"
Ethos	Ethics	Credibility (whether the speaker is believable to the audience) • Trustworthiness • Competence • Likeability
Pathos	Pathetic, Sympathy, Empathy	Appeal to feelings • Simple feelings (love) • Complex feelings (patriotism)

Figure 15.1: Modes of persuasion

morning, some listeners would go outside to check. So do everything in your control to establish your credibility.

What is in your control? You can mention your relevant experience in your introduction or early in the body of your speech (competence). You can conversationally make clear the source of your information (competence and trustworthiness). You can quote from experts who agree with your opinion (competence and trustworthiness). You can make clear your own motivations for asking the audience to accept your proposal (trustworthiness). You can bring up anything that legitimately establishes rapport with your audience—similar hobbies or interests, overlaps in experience, stories that establish your common humanity (likeability). Think in terms of the three components of *ethos*.

What can you *not* control? The list is practically endless. It could be something as innocuous and yet as psychologically damaging as having a similar appearance to a former employee who embezzled from your prospects. Since by definition you cannot control these factors, give your attention to the factors you **can** control so that you can compensate for the factors you **cannot**.

While establishing your credibility, you must at the same time appeal to the intellect and the emotions of your audience. We will consider the timing of such appeals more as we discuss Monroe's Motivated Sequence. For now, consider why you need both, especially in a speech designed to move your audience to action.

One of the authors remembers a class he taught some years ago at Murray State University. He asked the class how many of them believed seat belts save lives. (Note: this was years before seat belt laws.) About three-quarters of the class (15 people) raised their hands. He then asked how many of them actually buckled up every time they got in their cars. Only two raised their hands. The first group was intellectually convinced; the last group was motivated to action.

If you only have logical proof, you will only engage the intellect, which may work fine if your purpose is simply to convince. However, if you want to move them, you must involve "that which moves," i.e., the emotions. Most people, when asked, will say they believe they would be healthier if they exercised more. It's hard to find someone who says, "I would be healthier if I exercised less." However, relatively few people ever actually start and continue a real program of exercise. Many people who do so only start **after** something happens to make their own health needs "real" rather than abstract—the death of a close relative, dangerous shortness of breath when climbing stairs, or that first heart attack.

On the other hand, if you only have emotional proof, you may stir up an audience that will then fail to follow through. Some organizations that raise funds by means of highly-charged emotional television campaigns (remember some shocking photographs of starving children in foreign countries) often get high levels of pledges during their programs. But when the first of the month comes and the contributors have cooled off, if they cannot remember a reason to send their checks in, they will not do so.

Logos convinces us. *Pathos* moves us to action. *Logos* gives us a reason to keep moving.

Audience Analysis and Strategy

When you understand the audience's interest, understanding, and attitude toward your subject, you can begin to make some general plans about how to mix *ethos, logos,* and *pathos* to effectively appeal to them.

For instance, if you face an audience with no opinion because they are unfamiliar with your topic, you have a lot of basic informing to do before you can persuade them. However, you don't get any more time for your speech. So along with spending a lot of your speech telling them fact A, fact B, and fact C, you may need to scale back on the action you seek from your speech. For instance, your specific purpose may be: "I want my audience members to reduce red meat in their diets in order to reduce their blood cholesterol levels." It's unlikely that in one five-minute speech you will be able to effect such a drastic change, so you may change your specific purpose to read, "I want my audience members to get their blood cholesterol levels checked." Focus on what you can accomplish in the time allotted.

> **The challenge is often simply to get the audience members to hear you!**

On the other hand, your audience may have no opinion because they are apathetic, i.e., they don't care about the subject of your speech. Usually, this means they do not see the topic as having anything to do with them. A group of high school students who view cholesterol as an "old person's problem" may know a lot about the subject but not care about it. The approach here will be to show them early in the speech the relevance to their own lives, perhaps through a story or some other supporting material that appeals more to *pathos* than to *logos*.

Imagine giving a speech based on the specific purpose "I want my audience members to reduce red meat in their diets in order to reduce their blood cholesterol levels" to a group of hog farmers! If they don't walk out when they hear your purpose, they will mentally (and perhaps audibly) argue with everything you say. The difficulty here is simply to get them to listen!

In contrast with the usual academic approach of advancing a thesis and then offering proof (sometimes called the *deductive approach*), the indirect approach (also called the *inductive approach*) can be used profitably with any audience, but especially so with the strongly hostile audience (such as the hypothetical hog farmers). The idea is *not* to fool them into thinking you are on the same "side" ("I'm going to tell you six new recipes for sausage"). Rather, present your evidence *first*, followed by the points you have "proven." Once each point has been thus presented, you can tie them all together and then present your conclusion.

Monroe's Motivated Sequence

In the mid-1930s, Alan H. Monroe developed a pattern for persuasive messages that has become something of a standard because of its effectiveness. It is both logically and psychologically sound. It is known as the motivated sequence. Since it is explicitly designed to move an audience to action, it works well as both a strategy and an organizational pattern for a speech to actuate. Note: Where logos and pathos are discussed below, understand that these are generalities and are not meant to imply the exclusive use of those modes in the places indicated, but rather tendencies.

Attention: This step is designed to gain the interest of the listeners. One of the biggest problems here is assuming you have the audience's attention. In fact, assuming the step as given causes problems throughout the entire speech. You cannot persuade someone unless you have his or her attention.

This step is very similar to the traditional introduction.

Need: The need step is used for developing or describing some problem or for demonstrating that the audience has a need for the speech you are giving. You want them to say to themselves, "I need to hear this," or "Something needs to be done about this!" Again, don't assume the need is obvious. Remember that this step involves establishing the need from the standpoint of the audience member. The door-to-door salesperson who says "I need one more sale so I can go to Hawaii" is being ineffective; he should address the prospect's needs.

This step involves a lot of intellectual understanding and convincing, and so will need a solid dose of logos.

Satisfaction: Next, present a solution to the problem you presented in the Need step. Show how to satisfy the need. Scratch the itch. The Need step and the Satisfaction step appeal primarily to left-brained, logical thinking (although you always need some appeal to the right-brain thinking as well, especially in terms of clarifying information). In this step, you want the audience to think, "That will work!"

Again, this step will need logos for understanding and convincing.

Visualization: This is where we get into true persuasion. The purpose of this step is to develop within your audience an image of the consequences of their choices. If you want them to do something, you have to help them create in their minds an image of the good things that will happen if they do what you want them to do. Or, help them imagine the bad consequences of not adopting the policy.

In this step you are appealing more to right-brain thinking; you want to get them emotionally as well as logically involved, and you want them to feel those consequences on a gut level. In the Satisfaction step, you wanted them to think, "That will work." In the Visualization step, you want them to think, "That will work for me. I can do that. I can see myself doing that." Obviously there will be more appeal to pathos in this step as you seek to make carrying out your plan real to the audience on a "gut" level as well as an intellectual level.

Action: The action step should move your audience to actually do something about your speech. To do this, you need to have some clear and specific action for them to take. "Somebody should do something" only frustrates them, because they have no direction. Even "give some money to this cause" lacks motivation. Tell them, "I want each of you to give just $10 to this. If you can do more, fine. But don't you agree that $10 is within reach of all of us?" Or whatever it is you want them to do. You should know from the beginning of your speech what exact action you will ask them to take.

The action may or may not be identical to what you seek in your specific purpose. As exemplified earlier, your specific purpose may be: "I want my audience members to reduce red meat in their diets in order to reduce their blood cholesterol levels." The action you ask of them may be, "Go get your blood cholesterol levels checked." The action is designed to overcome the status quo and take advantage of inertia, rather than have inertia work against you. Since the status quo tends to remain the status quo, changing the status quo the least bit prior to ending your speech gets them moving in the right direction.

The Sales Talk

Although the most common persuasive situation is that of selling something to someone else in exchange for money, "selling" actually is part of everyone's life. You "sell" when you ask someone out on a date or to get married. You "sell" when you try to get a friend to attend the movie *you* prefer to see. You "sell" when you attempt to get your teenager to clean his room. Therefore, for our discussion, we will focus on applying persuasion in this way, recognizing that the skills involved in professional selling have a broad application outside that field.

By definition sales involves communication. Thus, it is not uncommon to see people skilled in communication do very well in all aspects of sales. Speech communication graduates have begun to find a great deal of success outside traditional sales positions, however. These positions include investment account executives, opinion research and census specialists, personnel managers, consultants in labor relations and in business administration, and to the U.S. government. Recently speech communication graduates have been highly visible in assisting lawyers in jury selection.

Using Sensory Devices in Selling

Selling a product is actually considered easier by many professionals in the sales world than selling an idea. When you sell a product, you have a tangible device and a built-in visual aid that will greatly assist you in your sales effort. Such sales talks have an inherent advantage over selling an idea because you don't have to rely so heavily on the imagination of your potential buyer(s), and in most cases, your potential buyer(s) can see the product and how it works and, therefore, be convinced to purchase the product. See how this works with Monroe's Motivated Sequence later in this chapter.

Ethos for Salespeople

In all persuasive efforts, you should make sure you are thoroughly familiar with the product or service you are trying to sell. You should know what the product is used for, how much it costs, and its **advantages** and **disadvantages** compared with competing products. Remember you should never criticize your competition but point out the advantages of your product over similar models. Learn far more about your product than you will ever need to know, including its weaknesses. Socrates called this the dialetic approach. Also, learn as much as you can about your product's competition. Be familiar with as much information about and relating to your product and competition as possible, so that you will be able to answer specific questions from a prospective buyer to help him or her make an educated and favorable decision about your product.

Purpose for the Sales Talk

The purpose of any sales presentation is, of course, "to make the sale." Your major objective is to prove and demonstrate how your product will meet the needs of your audience. Show how your product can make audience members' jobs easier, help them be more efficient, look better in the eyes of their superiors, ease work stress, etc. Simply put, "What's in it for the audience members?" if they purchase your product.

Audience Analysis in Sales

Understanding the demographic background of your audience members is essential in understanding what motivates them. Demographics can be defined as the social and economic background, age, race, religion, and any other data that help you better understand these people and adapt your talk to their needs and interests. See Chapter 5 for more on audience analysis.

Presenting Appeals for Sales

Addressing basic human needs is an important element in sales. What does the audience want and need?

What is it interested in? How much money is there to spend? What specific problems need to be solved? Understanding "Maslow's Hierarchy of Needs" is important in addressing the needs of potential buyers.

Abraham Maslow was a humanistic psychologist who proposed a five-tiered hierarchy to explain the motivations behind behavior (see Figure 15.2). Maslow's

Figure 15.2: Maslow's Hierarch of Needs (See accompanying CD for larger color illustration.)

*Self-Actualization Needs: realize potential, grow and develop as a person, seek challenges, curiosity, variety, success, independence, enjoyment

contribution was two-fold: 1) arranging human needs into a hierarchy, and 2) separating out self-actualization needs and placing them at the pinnacle. According to Maslow, in general, lower (or more basic) needs must be satisfied to at least a reasonable level before the higher level needs can even manifest themselves.

You may have studied this in another class. In this class, we want to see how we can use the concept to help us be more effective persuaders.

The needs include:

Physiological needs. These are the most basic survival needs such as food, water, air, shelter. It also includes the need for a reasonably comfortable environment. For example, people find it difficult to keep their minds on things when they are too hot or cold. We take the satisfaction of these needs for granted in our culture (with definite exceptions), but keep in mind that we are talking about psychological motivation.

Many people who have not gone hungry in years may still be haunted by experiences from childhood during the depression or World War II, and so be motivated by the fear of loss in this area. You may also be able to appeal here by arousing an awareness of a lack that audience members didn't know about prior to your speech.

Speech topics that have appealed to this need include: "The Nutritional Value of Whole Grain Breads" and "Will You Always Have Enough Pure Water to Drink?"

> **The appeal has more to do with whether people *feel* safe than whether they *are* safe.**

Safety/security needs. This is the need to be free from threats or predators, and the need to have life run smoothly (a very unsatisfied need in our society, especially among college students). This includes appeals to the need for safety and control as well as to tradition.

Again, the appeal has more to do with whether people *feel* safe than whether they *are* safe. At one point my parents, still living in the small town where I grew up and which had not experienced a murder in over three years, paid hundreds of dollars to have bars put on their windows. The daily circus presented by tabloid television had convinced them the world was much more dangerous than experience might suggest.

Speech topics that have appealed to this need include: "Some Practical Advice for Coping With Tornadoes" and "The Role of Superstitions in Our Lives." The latter topic helps illustrate how humans are motivated by needs rather than sheer reason. I don't consider myself superstitious. However, the speaker mentioned the superstition that for it to be lucky to pick up a penny, the penny has to be heads up. Somehow I managed to get well into adulthood without hearing the "heads up" part. Even though I'm not superstitious, I find myself picking up the heads-up pennies and leaving the tails-up ones on the basis of "Why take chances? It's just a penny." As one of my professors used to say, "People are not logical, they are *psycho*logical."

Belongingness and love needs. This area includes the need for satisfying relationships with other people, the need for acceptance, and the need to be part of a group. Political campaigns often appeal here via the bandwagon effect. In general it includes the need for friendship, nurturance, and sexual gratification.

When soft drink ads say things like "Join the Pepsi Generation," they're appealing to belongingness and love needs. Dr. Pepper's jingle once included the lines: "I'm a Pepper, he's a Pepper, she's a Pepper, we're a Pepper, wouldn't you like to be a Pepper too?" In this, Dr. Pepper managed to appeal to both the bandwagon effect and the need to be independent (which we'll discuss below) with the phrase "I'm part of an original crowd." The logical contradiction inherent in "original crowd" matters not; remember, "People are not logical, they are *psycho*logical."

Speech topics that have appealed to this need include: "How to be Popular on Campus" and "Get Involved: Volunteer Through Campus Organizations."

Esteem needs. The need for esteem is the need to have others look up to you. It includes the need to be respected by others and recognized by others (praise, status symbols, etc.). We can sum it up as the need to be treated as a valuable and important person. Independence and success are valued here as well as in self-actualization, but with a different flavor. See the discussion under the next heading for the difference.

It's worth pointing out that esteem needs come only after belongingness needs are satisfied to a reasonable degree. This helps explain why we'll do almost any boneheaded thing to be accepted by other teenagers. Only after we're accepted do we concern ourselves with whether others look up to us. First, we want to make sure they look at us at all.

Speech topics that have appealed to this need include: "My Ancestors Didn't Come Over on the Mayflower, But I'm a Pretty Important Person in My Own Right." (The idea was to be proud of where you come from, regardless of where it was, so that others would look up to you.)

Self-actualization needs. This area comprises the need to develop and grow as a person, to find one's identity, or to fully realize one's potential. It also includes the need to achieve satisfaction by a personal standard of excellence (as opposed to whether someone else thinks you have achieved excellence). Success and independence are valued here, but differently than under esteem needs. Under esteem needs we're concerned about whether other people believe we're successful and independent. Under self-actualization needs, we're concerned about whether we ourselves feel successful and independent by our own standards.

When I worked in the advertising department in the headquarters of Wal-Mart Stores, I noticed that Sam

Walton (at that time the richest man in America, according to *Forbes* magazine) drove an old, beat-up pickup truck—not a fancy restored older model, mind you, but one with dents and rust spots. Mr. Sam didn't really care if the neighbors thought he was successful or not. He had already met his esteem needs, and at that point in his life cared about meeting his own standards of excellence rather than someone else's.

The Army's advertisements in the past have appealed here ("Be all that you can be. Find your future in the Army"), as well as the Marines ("We're looking for a few good men"). Strangely enough, a lot of beer ads appeal here. When Red Dog brand came into our market, beer commercials on billboards read "You are your own dog."

Speech topics that have appealed to this need include: "Expand Your Horizons" and "Get the Most Out of Life by Realizing Your Dreams."

Applying Maslow

Every sales person should ask herself how her product can give her audience members (whether the audience comprises one or a thousand) greater health, self-respect, or happiness? In your sales presentation, focus on what your product can do for the prospective consumer rather than on how great the product itself is. Since you can appeal to almost any level of Maslow's Hierarchy with almost any product, make sure you understand what the customer wants from the product or service. In other words, describe your product in terms of potential consumer or buyer benefits. Expressing with positive wording the advantages of your product in terms of buyer benefits can be an effective technique for persuading the audience members that they should buy your product.

It should be obvious that we mean actual benefits, by the way. Don't say the car will fly when it won't.

Planning the Sales Talk

The sales talk is essentially the same as a strong persuasive speech. The sales talk is designed initially by developing a topical outline consisting of an introduction, body, and conclusion (see Chapter 9).

The Product as Your Best Visual Aid

A sales talk is generally very dependent on visual aids. As discussed in Chapters 12 and 17, you are your own best visual aid, so pay attention to your nonverbal "costuming" and, of course, product presentability. As a seller you should dress (costume) as though you don't need the sale. This is also one of the major philosophies of job interviewing. Dress as though you don't need the job. However, keep in mind your audience members and their demographics. For example, you probably wouldn't want to dress in a three-piece suit when giving a sales talk to a group of farmers interested in purchasing a John Deere tractor. Part of costuming is meeting audience expectations.

In your sales talk, arouse the interest of the audience by stating your primary appeal, by identifying and showing the product, and by stating briefly and showing *what the product can do for the listeners*. Also, give the audience a preview of the body of your talk by mentioning the main points you plan to discuss. In this way you will be helping the audience to listen actively throughout your presentation. Using and showing visuals in your talk may vary, depending on your product, your audience members and their specifications, the environment, and whether or not your presentation has been solicited.

We'd like to stress once again that selling is a *communication* process. It involves a *transaction*, i.e., a back-and-forth. Good presentations are based on good research. Good speaking must involve effective listening. Too many salespeople charge in with a solution before they have done any probing of the problem. A doctor who prescribes medication prior to diagnosing commits malpractice. So is a salesperson who tries to close before analyzing the situation. Persuasion starts well before you start talking.

The selling of your first product will be an exciting experience if you follow the suggested guidelines. However, these guidelines may be modified depending on the product and the audience. Sales can be an exciting profession. Happy hunting!

Study questions
1. What is ethos as it relates to sales?
2. Which is normally easier to do, sell an idea or sell a product? Why?
3. What are audience or client demographics?
4. Explain how Maslow's Hierarchy is important in presenting a sales pitch and addressing the needs of a potential client?

Chapter 16

Listening Skills

Communication is the transmission or exchange of symbols that stand for ideas or information. Intentional communication is initiated when a person has a message to transmit or convey to another person. The message is translated from thoughts into words (which are simply symbols for ideas). These symbols are then transmitted to the receiver. The receiver in turn interprets or adds meaning to the symbols heard or read.

"I know you believe you understand what you think I said, but I am not sure you realize that what you heard is not what I meant."

For true communication to take place, the symbols must represent the same or similar ideas to the receiver as they do to the sender in order for the receiver to understand the intended message. If for any reason the receiver does not comprehend the message the sender intends to relate, the communication process is not complete.

There are several reasons for reflecting or paraphrasing another person's words:

- Most of us have developed the habit of tuning in and out frequently as someone else talks (excursioning). Sometimes we can miss an important part of what is being said.
- Our mind speed (500 - 750 words per minute) greatly exceeds speech speed (100 - 150 wpm). So we may jump ahead to what we think the other person is going to say, or start developing our own reply.

- We can easily mishear or misinterpret what the other person is saying because (a) words can be ambiguous and (b) words can mean different things to different people.
- The other person may not be sure of what he/she is saying.

It is not always necessary to use reflective listening:

☐ Sometimes real understanding just isn't crucial.
☐ Sometimes the other person doesn't want to clarify what he/she is saying.
☐ Occasional vagueness is necessary to reach a useful compromise or consensus.
☐ In emergency situations there may be no time to check understanding.

Reflective listening is particularly valuable when:

√ The topic is important.
√ Action is to be taken based on the conversation.
√ You feel angry about what the other person is saying.
√ You are inclined to ignore, reject, or strongly disagree with what the other person is saying.
√ The other person keeps repeating or insisting on what he/she is saying.

Listening to Others

Below are listed some tips on listening. How many of them do you have trouble with? How many of them can you adapt to the speaker's point of view?

1. **WANT TO LISTEN.** Almost all problems in listening can be overcome by having the right

attitudes. Remember, there is no such thing as uninteresting people, only disinterested listeners.

2. **ACT LIKE A GOOD LISTENER.** Be alert, sit straight, lean forward if appropriate, let your face radiate interest.

3. **LISTEN TO UNDERSTAND.** Do not listen just for the sake of listening; listen to gain a real understanding.

4. **REACT.** The only time a person likes to be interrupted is when applauded. Be generous with your applause. Make the other person feel important. Applaud with nods, smiles, comments, and encouragement.

5. **STOP TALKING.** You can't listen while you are talking (neither can the person you are talking to). Communicate. Don't just take turns talking.

6. **EMPATHIZE WITH THE OTHER PERSON.** Try to put yourself in the other's place so that you can see her point of view.

7. **ASK QUESTIONS.** When you don't understand, when you need further clarification, when you want the other person to like you, when you want to show you are listening, ask questions. Make sure you don't *interrupt* with a question (unless the speaker has said that interruption is appropriate), and try not to ask questions that may embarrass the other person.

8. **CONCENTRATE ON WHAT THE OTHER PERSON IS SAYING.** Actively focus your attention on the words, the ideas, and the feelings related to the subject.

9. **LOOK AT THE OTHER PERSON.** The use of face, mouth, eyes, and hands all help the other person communicate with you. This helps you

concentrate and shows you are listening.

10. **SMILE APPROPRIATELY.** But don't overdo it.

11. **LEAVE YOUR EMOTIONS BEHIND** (if you can). Try to push your worries, your fears, and your problems away. They may prevent you from listening well.

12. **GET RID OF DISTRACTIONS.** Put down any papers, pencils, or other things you have in your hands; they may distract your attention.

13. **GET THE MAIN POINTS** (the big story). Concentrate on the main points and not the illustrative material; examples, stories, statistics, and other support are important, but usually they are not the main points. Examine them to see if they prove, support or define the main points.

14. **SHARE RESPONSIBILITY FOR COMMUNI-CATION.** Only part of the responsibility rests with the speaker; you as the listener have an important part to play. Try to understand, and if you don't, ask for clarification.

15. **REACT TO IDEAS, NOT TO THE PERSON.** Don't allow your reactions to the person influence your interpretation of words. Good ideas can come from people whose looks or personality you don't like.

16. **DON'T ARGUE MENTALLY.** When you are trying to understand the other person, it is a handicap to argue mentally while you are listening. This sets up a barrier between you and the speaker. Try to understand the whole idea before picking it apart.

17. **USE THE DIFFERENCE IN RATE.** You can listen faster than anyone can talk, so use this rate difference to your advantage by trying to stay on

the right track. Think back over what the speaker has said and connect it rather than drifting into unrelated thoughts.

18. **DON'T ANTAGONIZE THE SPEAKER.** You may cause the other person to conceal ideas, emotions, or attitudes by being antagonizing in any of a number of ways: arguing, criticizing, taking notes, not taking notes, asking questions, not asking questions, etc. Try to discern and be aware of the effect you are having on the other person. Adapt to the speaker.

19. **AVOID HASTY JUDGMENTS.** Wait until all the facts are in before making any judgments.

20. **LISTENING IS FUN!** Develop this attitude. Make a game of seeing how well you can listen.

21. **SEEK FIRST TO UNDERSTAND, THEN BE UNDERSTOOD.** Doing so makes it far more likely that you *will* understand, and it encourages the other person to try to understand you.

Apparent overstressing listening skills is important in any speech class because so much speaking is performed. As the old adage says: "The good Lord meant for us to listen twice as hard as He meant for us to talk. That's why He gave us two ears and one tongue."

Measuring Listening Skills

Communication is the transmission and exchange of ideas or information. Communication is a two way process. A message must be sent as well as received; thus, communication is circular. If for any reason the receiver does not comprehend the message the sender intends to relate, the communication process is not complete. If there is any interruption in this cycle, communication theorists call it "communication static". The communication cycle can be very powerful or fragile depending on the amount of communication static.

Hence, communication is a process, not just an event. Communication static can be identified as background noise, words with different meanings (slang, cliches and jargon), speaking delivery problems (i.e. diction, syntax, pitch, volume, rate, and pauses), and inefficient listening skills. The communication process is not complete until the message is received.

The following exercise can help enhance listening which can assist both the "speaker" (sender of the message) and "receiver" (destination of the message) to avoid communication static and contribute to more efficient transmission and exchange of information and ideas. The premise of reflective listening is simple. After having received the message (heard what you thought you understood the speaker say...), the receiver says: "[state the person's name] What I heard you say was....." The communication cycle is complete.

Now try reflective listening with a friend or classmate. The following tool will actually help you to measure the accuracy of your listening skills.

You should write a message of approximately 20 words in the "Sender's phone" and convey the message to your classmate and promptly cover the original message up with a sheet of paper. Next, the "Receiver's phone" performs "reflective listening" and writes the message down as the receiver perceived the message to read.

Now a comparison of the message sent and the message received is in order. Compare the original message to the message covered up by the sheet of paper. This measurement tool can be repeated several times for fun and practice for better listening skills. Have fun.

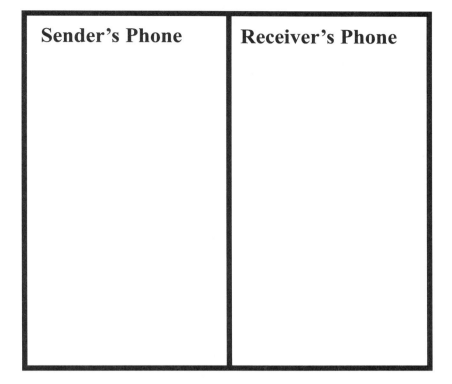

Sender's Phone	Receiver's Phone

Study questions
What is reflective listening?
What is active listening?
What is message static?
What are the most important guidelines for *you*
to improve *your* listening skills?

Chapter 17

Using Audio/visual Aids

Many speakers make a common mistake when they put together a speech: they don't speak to both brains. They don't use a visual aid. They forget to speak out to both the right brain and the left brain (Thompson & Paivio, 1994). The right brain, which seems to speed total comprehension when visuals are used, tends to help the left brain do a better job at analyzing and understanding what is being said (Bryden & Ley, 1983; Russell, 1979).

Play it safe—speak to both brains.

Brain Facts and Visuals

To better understand how professional audio/visual aids affect the listener, it is important for you to understand a few brain facts.

Characteristics of kinds of thinking
Right Brain
☐ Responds to feelings
☐ Has little sense of clock time
☐ Has a sense of space and understands spatial relationships
☐ Figures things out holistically through abstract thinking
☐ Draws or sketches
☐ Recognizes and remembers melodies and musical chords
☐ Uses parallel thinking in which the conclusion comes before or with the facts
☐ Uses metaphors to describe and define things
☐ Responds to visuals and colors

☐ Understands idiomatic language, which requires language pattern to understand

☐ Processes pictures

☐ Understands nonverbal behaviors and emotions

☐ Expresses emotions, moves, feels

☐ Is more physical

☐ Seeks patterns; takes pieces and puts into a whole or a pattern

☐ Thinks intuitively based on hunches, feeling, and emotions

Left Brain

■ Responds to facts

■ Has a sense of time and keeps track of time

■ Has a sense of order or chronology

■ Figures things out with linear, concrete, step-by-step thinking

■ Writes, reads music

■ Uses analytical thinking in which the conclusion comes after the facts

■ Uses speech and processes words

■ Uses names to describe and define things

■ Understands language, including grammar, syntax, and word meanings

■ Listens, talks, recites, is more cerebral

■ Analyzes; looks at parts of the whole

■ Thinks rationally based on facts and reasons and logic

Remember, one side of your brain is not better than the other side, just different from the other side.

Audio/Visuals

Audio/visual (A/V) aids include any materials you use (other than the words you speak) to enhance the audience's understanding of your presentation, to influence opinions, or to stimulate interest. Aids may include tables, graphs, diagrams, charts, objects, models, handouts, slides, drawings, photographs, phonographs, videotape or audio-tape, and anything else the audience can look at or listen to as a supplement to what you say.

Speeches with Visuals vs. Speeches Without

A/V aids should be an integral part of your overall presentation. They should help you get your points across to the audience and must add to rather than detract from your speech. Plan and develop your visual aids according to the purpose of your speech, the speech environment, and of course, the availability of materials and equipment. The aids you use in your speech should be designed appropriately and managed or handled during the presentation in such a way that they will be of optimum benefit to your audience.

Color Visual Aids vs. Black and White Visuals

Research shows that visuals or data presented in graphic form has better audience recall and is easier for your audience to understand. The graphic picture and verbal presentation combined increase listening speed comprehension (Zayas-Baya, 1977-78). Remember that the left brain focuses on more analytical processing of information and the right brain seems to help the brain speed and listening comprehension when pictures are used. If you use no visuals in your speech, you are putting a strain on the left

Figure 17.1: Level of listener retention of information when comparing color visual aids with that of black and white visuals (Vogel, Dickson, & Lehman, 1986).

High quality color visuals/ transparencies	Poor quality color and black and white visuals	Verbal presentation with no visual aids
20 % improved recall	13 % improved recall	5–10% normal recall without visual aids

195

brain. Therefore, deliver your presentation to your audience member's left and right brains to help them better understand and retain information presented in your two-brained speech.

Graphics

With current software, you can make your own graphics with minimal effort. You can produce them on laser printers, copy machines, or presentation software such as PowerPoint at your school production center.

Purpose Considerations

Informative. In planning audio/visual aids to enhance your presentation, consider whether your speech is primarily informative or primarily persuasive.

If you want to give your audience members information or teach them something, determine which points or aspects of that information will be most difficult for the listeners to grasp. Then develop one or more A/V aids that will help the audience see what you're talking about. For instance, your audience members will better grasp statistics and comparisons such as profit margins occurring over a five-year period if you use a table or graph. Your audience will have difficulty forming a mental picture of your speech if they only have your words to go on.

Make your information as easy as possible for the listeners to understand so that you can achieve your purpose quickly and thoroughly.

Persuasive. If the general purpose of your speech is persuasive (that is, if you are striving to convince the audience), design your visual aids to accomplish that result.

The audio/visual aids themselves can be persuasive and can even replace spoken words if you plan the aids carefully and use them effectively. A picture of a starving child will go a long way toward convincing people to contribute money to buy food for underprivileged children. Likewise, an audiotape of the music you are describing will give the audience a better feel for the music than just reading the words or describing the type of sound.

Time the elements of your speech to convince so they will have the desired impact on your listeners' memorable conclusion.

Speech Environment

You may be somewhat limited in the types of visuals you can employ in your presentation because of the environment or facilities in which you make your speech. For example, if the room cannot be darkened, don't plan visuals that use an overhead, opaque, film or slide projector. If the room is crowded with furniture, you may be able to arrange chairs or tables for optimum audience viewing of certain types of aids.

The size of the room and the number of listeners present for your speech will influence the type of visual you use. Your visuals must not overpower the audience or the room; on the other hand, they must be large enough for all to see. Your audience should be able to view or hear your aid from the rear of the room. Determine where you will deliver your presentation and design your visual aids so that they will be suitable for the environment.

Availability of Materials and Support

It is best to always rehearse with your visuals and provide backups, if possible. The availability of materials, equipment or machinery, and personnel may limit the types of visual aids you can provide. Once you've determined your speech content and have identified which points or elements need clarification or emphasis, decide what types of aid would best achieve your purpose. Then investigate the availability of items you need to construct or display those aids. If you can't get the necessary items, you may need to change your plans. As long as you discover limitations well in advance and make the best possible use of whatever support *is* available, your presentation will be effective.

If you plan to use special equipment such as projectors or easels to show your aids, or use machinery for a demonstration, make arrangements well in advance of your speech to make sure these items are accessible when you need them. Don't wait until the last minute to attempt to reserve, borrow, or otherwise arrange for the use of equipment. If something is not available when you need it, the effect of your entire presentation may be at risk!

> **Imagine what would happen if the light bulb burned out. You would certainly appear unprepared and would likely lose your confidence.**

Immediately before your speech, make sure that all materials are ready to use and that all equipment is ready and in good working order. Imagine what would happen if ten minutes into your presentation, as you are making a crucial point, you turned on the overhead projector to show a transparency and discovered that the light bulb had burned out. You would certainly appear unprepared and would likely lose your confidence.

Remember to rehearse your speech with your audio/visual aids. It is recommended that you rehearse your speech 15 or more times to adequately prepare your speech presentation.

The availability or willingness of people to help you manage your A/V aids may also influence which aids are feasible for your speech. For instance, you may need a helper to operate the machine and the room lights if you plan to use an opaque projector. This also promotes audience involvement—something that is usually positive. If you were to try doing these yourself during the presentation, you might distract the audience and disrupt the continuity of your speech. You may need someone to distribute handouts for you to a large audience. For a demonstration you may need someone to turn on a machine or perform some other task to ensure a smooth presentation and help keep the audience's attention on you and on your message.

If you anticipate needing the assistance of another person, **consult prospective volunteers well in advance of your presentation**.

Design

Constructing your visuals will help you connect with your audience. Whether you design your audio/visual aids yourself or use items prepared by someone else, they should be of suitable size, layout, and complexity. They should be designed so you can handle them with ease and confidence and so the audience can view them without much effort from the back of your classroom.

To determine whether an aid is of appropriate size for your speech, consider the dimensions of the presentation room and the number of people likely to be present. The people farthest away from you must be able to see and hear all pertinent details. On the other hand, an aid must not be so large (or so loud) that it overpowers the room and overwhelms the listeners.

If you design an audio/visual aid yourself, note that the color, the balance, and the general layout can enhance its overall attractiveness and visibility. Use vivid, dark colors to highlight items to which you want to draw the audience's attention (Wolf, Marsnik, Tracey, & Nichols, 1983). Borders around some visual aids may add to the visibility of important information as well as to the attractiveness and the interest of the items themselves. Any way that you can enhance the appeal of your visual aid will add to its effectiveness as an integral part of your speech. Remember, your audience's retention is better with color visuals than with black and white visuals, and a black and white visual is better for audience retention than no visual aid at all!

Audio/visual aids should not be so complex that the audience concentrates on interpreting the aid rather than understanding what you're saying. **Remember that an aid supplements your spoken words, so keep it simple. Don't attempt to provide more information on any single aid than the audience can grasp at a glance**. If your listeners must work to see or understand an A/V aid, it will distract more than help.

Management of Speech Tools

The manner in which you manage your audio/visual aid during presentations can influence greatly what effect the aids have on your audience. Research now shows that using some type of pointer to illustrate your visual aid actually helps listener retention.

When you present information from the lectern, it's helpful for your audience to perceive it as appealing. Make each reference to a visual aid a group experience by using the pointer when making specific points. If your audience members view your visual individually, they may not follow you logically. So illustrate and refer to specific elements of your visual as a group experience. Pointing out each concept to your audience as a group makes the information more appealing and fun.

Types of Acceptable Pointers
⇒retractable pointer
⇒ink pen
⇒pencil
⇒ruler
⇒dry board marker [pen]
⇒laser pointer (use in accordance to company regulations or abuse guidelines]

Note: be careful when using fingers, arms, etc. as pointers—you might send unintended mixed nonverbal messages to your audience.

Timing

Research shows that in general it is best to use your visual aid in the introduction of your speech. This concept closely parallels the "literary techniques"(listed in the beginning in Chapter 1). Use literary techniques in the beginning of your speech to obtain maximum audiences attention. Likewise, audio/visual aids should be used in your introduction.

However, revealing A/V aid at an inappropriate time can sometimes damage your presentation more than having no visual aids at all. In order to have a two-fold impact on the listeners, you need to reveal the aid to coincide with the audience's hearing relevant information (Perecman, 1983). **On your speech outline or note cards include a notation about when you plan to present an audio/visual aid so that you will not forget to use it** (see material in Chapter 13 on making effective speaking notes). During the presentation, display the aid when you refer to it and remove it from the audience's view when you're through talking about it.

Visibility

When referring to your visual aid, be sure the listeners have an unobstructed view of the item and display it long enough for them to grasp its significance. For instance, when pointing to a poster or chart on an easel, stand to the side of the easel, not between the audience and the aid. Try to face toward your audience, not toward the visual aid, when making your comments.

> **Generally, it is not advisable to pass an object around among your listeners because at least a few people at a time will be distracted from your message.**

When holding up an item for the listeners to look at, display it long enough and hold it high enough for all to see.

Generally, it is not advisable to pass an object around among your listeners because at least a few people at a time will be distracted from your message. As an alternative, invite the audience to examine objects and ask questions when your speech is finished.

The best way you can ensure your competent handling of visual aids during a speech is to **practice using your visuals when you rehearse the entire presentation**.

Professional Video and Audio Quick Check Question and Answers Session
1. What is the purpose of my A/V aid?
    *   To help explain or clarify a point (evidence).
    *   To give information.
    *   To establish credibility.
    *   To engage the senses of the audience.
    *   To emphasize a point.

- To set a mood.
- To gain the audience's attention (interest step—literary technique).

2. Technical considerations
   - Do you have time to get it?
   - Do you have the money to invest in it?
   - Can you handle it with ease and confidence?
   - Will you need help to set it up or use it?
   - Will you be able to use it in the speaking place?
   - Will it be available when you need it?
   - Will it violate any rules or regulations of the speaking venue?
   - Check spelling and double check (use a dictionary)

3. Day of the speech check list
   - Check to see that the equipment is working.
   - Bring extra batteries, light bulbs, etc.
   - Double check with any person who will be helping you.
   - Arrive early and set it up.
   - Practice with it.

4. Management
   - Show it at the right time.
   - Show it for the right amount of time.
   - Place the item for optimum effect.
   - Position yourself so that the audience can see it.
   - Handle it with ease and confidence.
   - Use a pointer, pen, pencil, ruler, etc. (Avoid pointing with your finger as this may send mix nonverbal messages that are inconsistent with your purpose).

5. Design
   - Consider the impact and meaning associated with color
   - Make it large enough to be seen in the back (the rear) of the auditorium, classroom.
   - Choose the amount of information that will keep it clear.
   - Consider the arrangement of the information to be consistent with your meaning. What is emphasized?
   - Keep it neat and clean.

6. Types of visual aids
   - Animal.
   - Art work (sculpture, painting).
   - Article.
   - Banner.
   - Banner in the air.
   - Bumper sticker.
   - Costume.
   - Demonstration.
   - Diorama.
   - Drama.
   - Flannel graph.
   - Fliers.
   - Flip charts.
   - Food.
   - Game.
   - Graphs/diagrams.
   - Makeup.
   - Map.
   - Model.
   - Object.
   - Overhead transparency.

- Pattern.
- Personal photograph.
- Plant.
- Sample.
- Scent.
- Sign.
- Slides.
- Sounds.
- Special lighting.
- Tapes.
- Video/film.
- Writing on the board (use with caution).
- **Power Point (rehearse with the system in the classroom or meeting room to make sure your presentation is compatible with the system).**

Study questions
1. Define what an audio/visual aid is. How will it help enhance your speech?
2. List several types of audio/visual aids.
3. When should you set up your visual aid?
4. When should you reveal your audio/visual aid?
5. Should you rehearse the speech with an audio/visual aid? Why or why not?

Works Cited in Chapter
(and Related References)

Annett, M. (1970). A classification of hand preference by association analysis. *British Journal of Psychology 61*:303-321.

Barnsley, R.H. and S.M. Ravinovitch. (1970). Handedness: Proficiency versus stated preference. *Perceptual and Motor Skills 30*:343-362.

Branch, C., B. Milner and T. Rasumssen. (1964). Intracarotid sodium amytal for the lateralization of cerebral speech dominance: Observation on 123 patients. *Journal of Neurosurgery 21*:399-405.

Bryden, M.P., & Ley, R.G. (1983). Right hemispheric involvement in imagery and affect. In E. Perecman (Ed.)., *Cognitive processing in the right hemisphere* (pp. 116-117). New York: Academic Press.

Fisher, R.S., M.P. Alexander, C. Gabriel, E. Gould and J. Milione. (1991). Reversed lateralization of cognitive functions in right handers. *Brain 114*:245-261.

Holder, M.K. (1992). Hand preference questionnaires: One gets what one asks for. M.Phil. thesis, Department of Anthropology, Rutgers University, New Brunswick, NJ, USA.

Perecman, E. (Ed.) (1983). *Cognitive processing in the right hemisphere.* New York: Academic Press.

Rasmussen, T. and B. Milner. (1977). Clinical and surgical studies of the cerebral speech areas in man. In: Zulch, K.J., O. Creutzfeltd and G.C. Galbraith (eds.), *Cerebral localization.* NY: Sringer Verlag, pp. 238-255.

Ross, E.D. (1984). Right hemisphere's role in language, affective behavior and emotion. *Trends in Neuroscience* 7:3342-346.

Schiller, F. (1979). *Paul Broca: Founder of French anthropology, explorer of the brain.* Berkeley, CA: University of California Press.

Thompson, V.A., & Paivio, A. (1994). Memory for pictures and sounds: Independence of auditory and visual codes. *Canadian Journal of Experimental Psychology, 48*(3), 380395.

Vogel, D. R., Dickson, G. W., & Lehman, J. A. (1986). Persuasion and the role of visual presentation support: The UM/3M study (in-house publication, pp. 1-1-20). St. Paul, MN: 3M Corporation.

Wada, J. and T. Rasmussen. (1960). Intracarotid injection of sodium amytal for the lateralization of cerebral speech dominance. *Journal of Neurosurgery 17*:266-282.

Wernike, C. (1874). Der Aphasische Symtomenkomplex. Eine Psychologische Studie auf Anatomischer Basis. Breslau: M. Cohn und Weigart. Reprinted in *Wernicke's works on aphasia: A source book and review*, translated by G. E. Eggert, 91-144. The Hague, Netherlands: Mounton Publishers, 1977.

Wolff, F. I., Marsnik, N. C., Tracey, W. S., & Nichols, R. G. (1983). *Perceptive listening.* New York: Holt, Rinehart & Winston.

Zayas-Baya, E. P. (1977-78). Instructional media in the total language picture. *International Journal of Instructional Media 5*, 145-150.

Chapter 18

Bonus Material and Appendices

How *Not* To Act At An Interview

These suggestions are compiled from Vic Blocher's speech students, based on their own observations, experiences, and overheard horror stories.

1. Do not undress.
2. Do not spit, smoke, or chew gum or tobacco.
3. Do not be late.
4. Do not go extremely high or trashed.
5. Do not go in with cell phone or pager.
6. Do not fall asleep or yawn.
7. Do not forget to bathe, brush, shower, or shave.
8. Do not slouch.
9. Do not ever belch or break wind.
10. Do not use improper English.
11. Do not avoid questions.
12. Do not go unprepared.
13. Do not forget a copy of your resumé.
14. Do not take kids, pets, or friends.
15. Do not park in the president's parking spot.
16. Do not assume anything.
17. Do not laugh at every joke.
18. Do not adjust clothing or become fidgety.
19. Do not over compliment interviewer.
20. Do not ask why you are here.
21. Do not fail to show up.
22. Do not walk out to use bathroom.
23. Do not say "Huh?" or "What?"

24. Do not be shy, quiet, or informal.
25. Do not forget to use breath mints before interview.
26. Do not discuss personal topics.
27. Do not use too much cologne, perfume, or makeup.
28. Do not act disinterested or overly interested.
29. Do not play games (mind games, name games, etc.).
30. Do not ask interviewer questions unrelated to the job.

Job Interview Communication Skills

☐ **Assess your skills and abilities.** Ask yourself "What can I do?" "What have I done?"

☐ **Identify the needs of the employer.** Focus on what the employer values and wants.

☐ **Listen, respond, ask questions.** Anticipate typical questions; project a positive attitude during the interview.

☐ **Follow up after the interview.** Write thank-you notes; help your references send meaningful recommendation letters.

Measuring Speechfright

To demonstrate that your speechfright symptoms will diminish considerably by the end of the semester, we have devised a measurement to help you assess yourself.

Note: Do not fill this out at the beginning of the term. See directions for usage.

Directions:

1. In the five spaces below, write your most noticeable speechfright symptoms.
2. Rate each symptom on a scale of 1–10 (the maximum amount of discomfort would rate a 10; the least amount would rate a 1).
3. At the beginning of the term turn to the similar form in Chapter 2 (First speech) and fill it out. Fill this one out at the end of the term, then compare this one and that one to see the difference.

Initial observed symptom	Rating
1. _____	_____
2. _____	_____
3. _____	_____
4. _____	_____
5. _____	_____

Warm-up Exercise

Just as athletes and musicians warm-up before performing, you will find it helpful to loosen up before speaking.

The following exercise is a good warm-up for speakers, especially for anyone who has trouble pronouncing English vowels and consonants.

Practice this articulation exercise, making sure your mouth is open wide enough to insert three or four fingers vertically. Round all vowel sounds (A,E,I,O,U) and attack each consonant sound.

After you have mastered **B**, try other consonants. **T**, **L**, **F**, **S**, and **W** are particularly challenging.

Remember: The challenge is to master the sound combinations with correct vowel and consonant articulation. The actual rhythm you use is comparatively unimportant.

B - A BAY	**L - A LAY**
B - E BEE	**L - E LEE**
B - I BICKEY	**L - I LICKEY**
BYE	**LYE**
B - O BOW	**L - O LOW**
BICKEY BYE	**LICKEY LYE**
BOW	**LOW**
B - U BOO	**L - U LOO**
BICKEY BYE	**LICKEY LYE**
BOW BOO	**LOW LOO**

Tear-out Evaluations Forms

The next several pages are tear-out evaluation forms for you to give your teacher for use in giving you feedback. They are designed to fit into this textbook while giving maximum space for the instructor to give you feedback. Each sheet of paper has the "top" half of a form on the front and the "bottom" half of a form on the back. Be sure to check *both sides* for feedback when you get it back.

Patterns in My Speaking

This space is provided as a convenient place for you to look for patterns in your speaking, based on feedback from your instructor (and other sources such as classmates and your own observations). Do you see similar issues cropping up speech after speech? Here's an opportunity to become aware of those habits and patterns so you can make informed decisions about how to deal with them.

Public Speaking Evaluation
Form A

Name _____   Speech number _____

Purpose/subject
Appropriate
Clear
Researchable

Organization
Introduction:
Interesting
Effective
Body:
Clear organization
Effective evidence
Clear reasoning
Conclusion:
Clear summary
Effective final appeal

Form:
Outline
Works Cited

Style
Appropriate
Diction, syntax, grammar
Originality

Rehearsal

Adequate
Effective use of notes
Effective use of A/V aid

Delivery

Verbal:
Volume
Vocal variety
Emphasis/inflection
Tone/pitch
Rate/pauses
Articulation/pronunciation

Nonverbal:
Attitude
Eye contact/focus
Appearance
Posture
Positioning/movement
Gestures
Use of lectern

Overall Effect

Original
Clear
Interesting

Grades/comments

Public Speaking Evaluation
Form A

Name _____ Speech number _____

Purpose/subject

Appropriate

Clear

Researchable

Organization

Introduction:

Interesting

Effective

Body:

Clear organization

Effective evidence

Clear reasoning

Conclusion:

Clear summary

Effective final appeal

Form:

Outline

Works Cited

Style

Appropriate

Diction, syntax, grammar

Originality

Rehearsal

Adequate
Effective use of notes
Effective use of A/V aid

Delivery

Verbal:
Volume
Vocal variety
Emphasis/inflection
Tone/pitch
Rate/pauses
Articulation/pronunciation

Nonverbal:
Attitude
Eye contact/focus
Appearance
Posture
Positioning/movement
Gestures
Use of lectern

Overall Effect

Original
Clear
Interesting

Grades/comments

Public Speaking Evaluation
Form A

Name _____   Speech number _____

Purpose/subject

Appropriate

Clear

Researchable

Organization

Introduction:

Interesting

Effective

Body:

Clear organization

Effective evidence

Clear reasoning

Conclusion:

Clear summary

Effective final appeal

Form:

Outline

Works Cited

Style

Appropriate

Diction, syntax, grammar

Originality

Rehearsal

Adequate
Effective use of notes
Effective use of A/V aid

Delivery

Verbal:
Volume
Vocal variety
Emphasis/inflection
Tone/pitch
Rate/pauses
Articulation/pronunciation

Nonverbal:
Attitude
Eye contact/focus
Appearance
Posture
Positioning/movement
Gestures
Use of lectern

Overall Effect

Original
Clear
Interesting

Grades/comments

Public Speaking Evaluation
Form A

Name _____

Speech number _____

Purpose/subject

Appropriate
Clear
Researchable

Organization

Introduction:
Interesting
Effective

Body:
Clear organization
Effective evidence
Clear reasoning

Conclusion:
Clear summary
Effective final appeal

Form:
Outline
Works Cited

Style

Appropriate
Diction, syntax, grammar
Originality

Rehearsal

Adequate
Effective use of notes
Effective use of A/V aid

Delivery

Verbal:
Volume
Vocal variety
Emphasis/inflection
Tone/pitch
Rate/pauses
Articulation/pronunciation

Nonverbal:
Attitude
Eye contact/focus
Appearance
Posture
Positioning/movement
Gestures
Use of lectern

Overall Effect

Original
Clear
Interesting

Grades/comments

Public Speaking Evaluation
Form A

Name _____ Speech number _____

Purpose/subject
Appropriate
Clear
Researchable

Organization
Introduction:
Interesting
Effective
Body:
Clear organization
Effective evidence
Clear reasoning
Conclusion:
Clear summary
Effective final appeal

Form:
Outline
Works Cited

Style
Appropriate
Diction, syntax, grammar
Originality

Rehearsal

Adequate
Effective use of notes
Effective use of A/V aid

Delivery

Verbal:
Volume
Vocal variety
Emphasis/inflection
Tone/pitch
Rate/pauses
Articulation/pronunciation

Nonverbal:
Attitude
Eye contact/focus
Appearance
Posture
Positioning/movement
Gestures
Use of lectern

Overall Effect

Original
Clear
Interesting

Grades/comments

Public Speaking Evaluation
Form A

Name _____

Speech number _____

Purpose/subject
Appropriate
Clear
Researchable

Organization
Introduction:
Interesting
Effective
Body:
Clear organization
Effective evidence
Clear reasoning
Conclusion:
Clear summary
Effective final appeal

Form:
Outline
Works Cited

Style
Appropriate
Diction, syntax, grammar
Originality

Rehearsal

Adequate
Effective use of notes
Effective use of A/V aid

Delivery

Verbal:
Volume
Vocal variety
Emphasis/inflection
Tone/pitch
Rate/pauses
Articulation/pronunciation
Nonverbal:
Attitude
Eye contact/focus
Appearance
Posture
Positioning/movement
Gestures
Use of lectern

Overall Effect

Original
Clear
Interesting

Grades/comments

Speaker Critique Form B

Speaker's Name: _____

Thesis Statement: _____

Type of Speech: _____

Date: _____

	Comments
Subject and purpose Suited to speaker? Suited to audience and occasion? Did you state your thesis?	
Introduction Use of humor? Interest, importance, icebreakers? Use of anecdotes, enthusiasm? Were you clear?	
Body Effective plan, logic, language? Were you credible, accurate? Researched sources cited? Variety of sources and certified? Adequate rehearsal, humor? Use of examples, analogies? Use of testimonials, creativity?	
Visuals Knowledgeable of equipment? Appropriate timing? Creativity and preparation?	

Conclusion

Clear and informative?
Sufficiently motivating, assertive?
Good appeal for action?
Restatement of thesis?

Oral Presentation

Confident, relaxed, poised?
Correct posture, eye contact?
Effective gestures? Smile?
Too dependent on notes?
Did you lean on the lectern?
Proper rate durations, breathy?
Effective pitch changes, volume?
Expressive tonal quality?
Distinct articulation?
Correct pronunciation? Slang use?

+(Favorable)   -(Needs improvement)

Miscellaneous:

Assigned time: _____ to _____ minutes
Time of your speech: _____ min. _____ sec.

SPEECH GRADE_____

Note: to equal or better this grade, subsequent speeches must improve. To demonstrate improvement, future speeches must show progress in the above indicated area(s).

Speaker Critique Form B

Type of Speech: _____

Speaker's Name: _____   Date: _____

Thesis Statement: _____

	Comments
Subject and purpose Suited to speaker? Suited to audience and occasion? Did you state your thesis?	
Introduction Use of humor? Interest, importance, icebreakers? Use of anecdotes, enthusiasm? Were you clear?	
Body Effective plan, logic, language? Were you credible, accurate? Researched sources cited? Variety of sources and certified? Adequate rehearsal, humor? Use of examples, analogies? Use of testimonials, creativity?	
Visuals Knowledgeable of equipment? Appropriate timing? Creativity and preparation?	

Conclusion

Clear and informative?
Sufficiently motivating, assertive?
Good appeal for action?
Restatement of thesis?

Oral presentation

Confident, relaxed, poised?
Correct posture, eye contact?
Effective gestures? Smile?
Too dependent on notes?
Did you lean on the lectern?
Proper rate durations, breathy?
Effective pitch changes, volume?
Expressive tonal quality?
Distinct articulation?
Correct pronunciation? Slang use?

+(Favorable)   -(Needs improvement)

Miscellaneous:

Assigned time: _____ to _____ minutes
Time of your speech: _____ min. _____ sec.

SPEECH GRADE _____

Note: to equal or better this grade, subsequent speeches must improve. To demonstrate improvement, future speeches must show progress in the above indicated area(s).

Speaker Critique Form B

Speaker's Name: _____

Type of Speech: _____

Date: _____

Thesis Statement: _____

Comments

Subject and purpose Suited to speaker? Suited to audience and occasion? Did you state your thesis?	
Introduction Use of humor? Interest, importance, icebreakers? Use of anecdotes, enthusiasm? Were you clear?	
Body Effective plan, logic, language? Were you credible, accurate? Researched sources cited? Variety of sources and certified? Adequate rehearsal, humor? Use of examples, analogies? Use of testimonials, creativity?	
Visuals Knowledgeable of equipment? Appropriate timing? Creativity and preparation?	

Conclusion

Clear and informative?
Sufficiently motivating, assertive?
Good appeal for action?
Restatement of thesis?

Oral presentation

Confident, relaxed, poised?
Correct posture, eye contact?
Effective gestures? Smile?
Too dependent on notes?
Did you lean on the lectern?
Proper rate durations, breathy?
Effective pitch changes, volume?
Expressive tonal quality?
Distinct articulation?
Correct pronunciation? Slang use?

+(Favorable)   -(Needs improvement)

Miscellaneous:

Assigned time: _____ to _____ minutes
Time of your speech: _____ min. _____ sec.

SPEECH GRADE _____

Note: to equal or better this grade, subsequent speeches must improve. To demonstrate improvement, future speeches must show progress in the above indicated area(s).

Speaker Critique Form B

Speaker's Name: _____

Thesis Statement: _____

Type of Speech: _____

Date: _____

	Comments
Subject and purpose Suited to speaker? Suited to audience and occasion? Did you state your thesis?	
Introduction Use of humor? Interest, importance, icebreakers? Use of anecdotes, enthusiasm? Were you clear?	
Body Effective plan, logic, language? Were you credible, accurate? Researched sources cited? Variety of sources and certified? Adequate rehearsal, humor? Use of examples, analogies? Use of testimonials, creativity?	
Visuals Knowledgeable of equipment? Appropriate timing? Creativity and preparation?	

Conclusion

Clear and informative?
Sufficiently motivating, assertive?
Good appeal for action?
Restatement of thesis?

Oral presentation

Confident, relaxed, poised?
Correct posture, eye contact?
Effective gestures? Smile?
Too dependent on notes?
Did you lean on the lectern?
Proper rate durations, breathy?
Effective pitch changes, volume?
Expressive tonal quality?
Distinct articulation?
Correct pronunciation? Slang use?

+(Favorable)   -(Needs improvement)

Miscellaneous:

Assigned time: _____ to _____ minutes
Time of your speech: _____ min. _____ sec.

SPEECH GRADE _____

Note: to equal or better this grade, subsequent speeches must improve. To demonstrate improvement, future speeches must show progress in the above indicated area(s).

Speaker Critique Form B

Speaker's Name: _____

Thesis Statement: _____

Type of Speech: _____

Date: _____

	Comments
Subject and purpose Suited to speaker? Suited to audience and occasion? Did you state your thesis?	
Introduction Use of humor? Interest, importance, icebreakers? Use of anecdotes, enthusiasm? Were you clear?	
Body Effective plan, logic, language? Were you credible, accurate? Researched sources cited? Variety of sources and certified? Adequate rehearsal, humor? Use of examples, analogies? Use of testimonials, creativity?	
Visuals Knowledgeable of equipment? Appropriate timing? Creativity and preparation?	

Conclusion

Clear and informative?
Sufficiently motivating, assertive?
Good appeal for action?
Restatement of thesis?

Oral presentation

Confident, relaxed, poised?
Correct posture, eye contact?
Effective gestures? Smile?
Too dependent on notes?
Did you lean on the lectern?
Proper rate durations, breathy?
Effective pitch changes, volume?
Expressive tonal quality?
Distinct articulation?
Correct pronunciation? Slang use?

+(Favorable)   -(Needs improvement)

Miscellaneous:

Assigned time: _____ to _____ minutes
Time of your speech: _____ min. _____ sec.

SPEECH GRADE _____

Note: to equal or better this grade, subsequent speeches must improve. To demonstrate improvement, future speeches must show progress in the above indicated area(s).

Speaker Critique Form B

Speaker's Name: _____

Thesis Statement: _____

Type of Speech: _____

Date: _____

Comments

Subject and purpose
Suited to speaker?
Suited to audience and occasion?
Did you state your thesis?

Introduction
Use of humor?
Interest, importance, icebreakers?
Use of anecdotes, enthusiasm?
Were you clear?

Body
Effective plan, logic, language?
Were you credible, accurate?
Researched sources cited?
Variety of sources and certified?
Adequate rehearsal, humor?
Use of examples, analogies?
Use of testimonials, creativity?

Visuals
Knowledgeable of equipment?
Appropriate timing?
Creativity and preparation?

Conclusion

Clear and informative?
Sufficiently motivating, assertive?
Good appeal for action?
Restatement of thesis?

Oral presentation

Confident, relaxed, poised?
Correct posture, eye contact?
Effective gestures? Smile?
Too dependent on notes?
Did you lean on the lectern?
Proper rate durations, breathy?
Effective pitch changes, volume?
Expressive tonal quality?
Distinct articulation?
Correct pronunciation? Slang use?

Miscellaneous:

+(Favorable)   -(Needs improvement)

Assigned time: _____ to _____ minutes
Time of your speech: _____ min. _____ sec.

SPEECH GRADE _____

Note: to equal or better this grade, subsequent speeches must improve. To demonstrate improvement, future speeches must show progress in the above indicated area(s).

Additional Material and Contact

Be sure to check the accompanying CD-ROM for color illustrations that go along with the text, additional practical information, links to online resources, and other materials.

Things change quickly in the modern world. We are already looking forward to the next edition of this textbook, and would appreciate your input. We have provided two or three means of contacting us, in the hope that at least one of them will be working at all times.

Online support page for updates to information: http://www.soapboxorations.com/rs/

E-mail address for one of the authors (who can pass on information to the others): dking@pstcc.edu

Snail-mail address if all else fails:

[one of our names]
Pellissippi State Technical Community College
Liberal Arts Department
PO Box 22990
Knoxville, TN 37933-0990

Index

243

E

easels 198
education xi
emotions 108. *See also* pathos
emphasis 124
energy
  harness 21
entertain 12, 48, 50–51
enthusiasm 55, 163
environment
  physical 56
  speaking 56
ethics 33
ethos 65, 121, 162, 167
eulogy 12
exaggeration 37
example 98
expert testimony 98
experts 169
extemporaneous 48, 139, 140. *See also* modes of delivery
  defined 139

F

facial expressions 125, 148
facial language. *See* nonverbal communication
ferry sinking 1
fight-or-flight 22–24
focus 28, 47
freezer car 2
furniture 128

G

general purpose 12
gestures 120
glycogen 22
green monkey principle 28, 55

H

hard support 155
hard supporting material 94. *See also* supporting material
Hawthorne, Nathaniel 24
headlines 109
Hitler, Adolph 107

I

idea
  transmission 2
impression formation 148
impromptu 139
indicators 128–129
inductive approach 172
inform 12, 48, 49, 151. *See also* instruct
  demonstrate 12, 48, 49
  teach 12
information 151
information overload 153
instruct 48, 151. *See also* inform
interest 42
Internet 67–68
interview 44, 68–69
  guidelines 69
introduction 78
Inuit 4

J

job interview tips 209, 210
judgment 35

K

kinesics 131
know subject 27–31
knowledge 42

L

lay testimony 101
likeability 163
Lincoln, Abraham 24
listening 185
  improving 186

R

rapport 169
referrals 157
relationships 157
repeat business 157
repetition 155
research 11, 14, 54, 65
responsibility 36
rhetoric 50
right brain/left brain. *See* bicameral
    mind

S

sales
    157, 175, 176, 181, 182, 183
sales talks 174–183
sample topics 58
scientific reports 97
selecting a topic 11
selling 157, 174, 175, 183
semantics 7
sensory devices 166
sentence
    as the basis of thought 82
sermonize 12
short-term memory 76–77
signposting 154
silent language. *See* nonverbal
    communication
silent messages. *See* nonverbal
    communication
simplicity 73–77
    vs. simplistic 73–74
Sioux 107
soft support 155
soft supporting material 96. *See*
    also supporting material
source 38
sources 57, 65
speaking outline 81. *See also* notes
speaking rate 57, 120, 146, 185
special occasion speech 52

specific purpose 12, 52–
    53, 75, 83
speechfright
    21, 23, 24, 26, 27, 28, 29
    handling 29–31, 55
stage fright. *See* speechfright
standards 33, 34, 35, 36
statements of fact 159
statements of policy 160
statements of value 159
statistics 93, 97
story. *See* narrative
subpoints 75
supporting material 93, 155
    examples 97
    major types 94
    need for both types 102
suppression of key information 39
symbol 2, 107, 121–122
symbols 73
symmetry 77–79

T

tape recorder 70, 110–111
testimonial 12
thematic statement. *See* thesis
thesis 11, 13, 14–15, 75, 84
timing 78
toast 12
topic 13, 47, 53
    criteria 13–14, 54, 58
transactional process 2
trustworthiness 162, 169
truth 34

U

understanding 152

V

value 48, 49
values 33–34
vicious cycle 25–26
visual aid 175
vivid language 112
vocalics 120. *See also*
    paralanguage
voice tone 147

W

warm hands 26
Washington, George 24
words 6
World's Smallest Political Quiz 74

Y

your own interests 54